Man a Society

D0411641

MAN VS OCEAN

THE INSPIRATIONAL STORY OF A TOASTER SALESMAN WHO SETS OUT TO SWIM THE WORLD'S DEADLIEST OCEANS AND CHANGE HIS LIFE FOR EVER

ADAM WALKER

797.21092

JOHN BLAKE

Published in Great Britain by
John Blake Publishing Limited
3 Bramber Court, 2 Bramber Road
London W14 9PB

www.johnblakebooks.com

www.facebook.com/johnblakebooks   ◼
twitter.com/jblakebooks   ◼

First published in hardback in 2016

ISBN: 978-1-78418-416-2

British Library Cataloguing-in-Publication Data:

A catalogue record for this book is available from the British Library.

Design by www.envydesign.co.uk

Printed in Great Britain by CPI Group (UK) Ltd

3 5 7 9 10 8 6 4 2

Papers used by John Blake Publishing are natural, recyclable products made
from wood grown in sustainable forests. The manufacturing processes conform
to the environmental regulations of the country of origin.

Every attempt has been made to contact the relevant copyright-holders,
but some were unobtainable. We would be grateful if the appropriate
people could contact us.

CONTENTS

I would like to dedicate this book to anyone who has ever had a dream and may feel it is unreachable or has been told it is unachievable. Believe, inspire, succeed!

AUTHOR'S NOTE

For the purposes of this book I have often referred to 'cold' water. Please note that this word doesn't exist in my mind, as it is negative and serves no positive purpose in the sport of open-water swimming. I would advise that you also erase it from your mind. Happy swimming! ☺

PROLOGUE

It feels like the end for me. In an instant I can feel the dream slipping away. This wasn't part of the master plan – this isn't how it is supposed to finish. My mind has gone into turmoil. All the training in the world couldn't have prepared me for this. My stomach is on fire, as if it's being scalded by a hot poker or cut open with a razor blade. I have trained myself to tolerate discomfort and pain, but this is a different level. Is this the ocean's way of testing me? I can hear it saying, 'You underestimated me. We are going to see how badly you want this and how capable you actually are.' Everything in my brain wants to stop and it's not like I have time to think about it – it is an instant reaction. My mind is computing what is happening to me and it wants out. I have been in situations many times before where I was on the edge of giving up in training, for various reasons including the cold, sickness, nosebleeds, stomach ache, headaches, physical and mental pain – sometimes having a number of these issues all at the same time. However, I have always managed to convince myself to carry on. This time is different – there is no negotiating with myself on this one. The swim is over.

I know this isn't acceptable, though, and that I wouldn't be able to live with myself knowing I had quit. There has to be another solution – I have to find a way to keep going.

I hadn't factored this situation into my thoughts. I had trained myself to believe in my mind that succeeding was the only outcome, and failure wasn't worth thinking about. But once you are going through an extreme situation, the game can change. Throughout these swims I had often wondered why failure was such a problem for me. Of course no one likes to fail in anything, and the fear of failure is often the reason people will not step outside their comfort zones and take a risk. In sport, throughout my growing years, I had hated not succeeding in everything I did. Not feeling I had done myself justice, which frustrated me. I so wanted to be a professional athlete, I craved it, knowing there are many children growing up who feel the same way but few who actually realise their dream. When you are a child it seems unachievable and those who do achieve it are often those who have been spotted, put on some talent-development programme and groomed to succeed. There is still a high percentage of incredible talents who don't get that chance to prove themselves and be counted.

I think my desire to succeed in this sport is a combination of being brought up to give it my all by my dad and another feeling, like redemption, from a career I was never passionate about. Succeeding at swimming represented fulfilling my childhood dream and getting a second chance. Maybe it was too late for a career in sport, due to my age, but I'd hoped it would at least plug a few gaps in my life and give me a more even balance.

I'm shouting with only a kayak next to me in the middle of the Pacific Ocean. I simply cannot help it. I try not to show any pain as I don't want to show weakness and allow it to have any power or meaning over me. I also cannot give the pilot or my team any reason to get me out. I have to mask how much trouble I'm in or the swim will be taken out of my hands. I try to tell my kayaker I'm OK and to give me a minute in-between shouting and clutching my stomach. I desperately don't want to make obvious the pain I am in, but it is like I have been possessed and something has taken over my body. I can't stop shouting.

I ask the kayaker how long to go, knowing it isn't going to be a few minutes but somehow wishing he'll give me a positive response. He replies, 'Oh, dude, it's about an hour.' I can hear in his voice that he thinks the swim is over and it doesn't matter what I say. He thinks it's the end of the swim and I'll be getting out.

I ask him to give me a minute as I tread water alone in the pitch-black sea. I don't know what is happening to me and what has done this. I don't dare move forward in case it happens again. I am in despair!

1
THE EARLY YEARS

This isn't going to be one of those stories about how, as a child, I was always destined to be an elite athlete and how I was winning national pool titles before I reached the age of ten, with my destiny written in swimming. The truth is I was a good county swimmer and I played a mixture of sports.

As a toddler I would sit on the bottom of the pool with my eyes open. I have a memory of doing this in the local swimming pool at a very early age, sending my poor grandma, nana and mum into distress as they thought I was going to drown. I have always liked it underwater – I find it peaceful away from everyday life. It is like a different world and there is a tranquillity that makes me happy.

In my teens I would grip onto the pool steps and see how long I could hold my breath for, endeavouring to beat my previous time. I have always been competitive like that; it doesn't matter what the challenge was – I would always strive to be better, especially when it came to sport.

At the age of seven I joined Bingham Swimming Club, which was less than ten minutes from my parents' house in Nottingham, England. For as long as I can remember I've loved to swim. I realised by the age of eight that I was best at backstroke, and this then became my chosen stroke for pool racing.

I had a terrible technique. I was no good at starts or turns and I would lift my head up and not lie back in the water like the conventional streamlined stroke. I would rely on my arms, which I would wind over as fast as possible in a windmill-like fashion until I touched the other side. No finesse, no real style – just as much power as I could muster.

I would compete in the local galas and regularly win the 50 metres backstroke. I enjoyed running into the lounge after my swim gala, excited to let my mum and dad know the outcome. I believe this competitive nature came from my dad.

He was brought up with a winning mentality, which also included standing up for yourself in difficult situations. It was instilled into him by his mother from the age of eleven, when he was sent to a boarding school and had to learn to fend for himself.

I remember him telling me the story of when he arrived at school. As part of the induction, the older boys would take the newcomers out on a rowing boat to the middle of a lake. They would push them in and tell them to swim back to shore.

My dad was not keen on this idea and wanted to set his stall out early, so the older boys knew he was not someone to be messed with. He proceeded to tell them, 'If anyone lays a hand on me then they will be going in as well!' At this response they thought better of it and left him alone, whereas all the other young starters had to swim back.

My dad played different sports and had a particular interest in cricket and rugby. Rugby was his favourite and he played it from the age of twelve to the age of forty-five. He played for Sheffield Tigers, which was a top club in the area, before he broke his ankle and was forced to retire. His position was prop forward and he was very competitive; he brought me up to play hard but fair.

I looked up to my dad growing up. He taught me to try to be a winner and was always saying, whatever it is in life, 'Give it everything you've got!' I would always hear his voice in my head before the start of a swimming race, saying this over and over again. This motivated me and gave me the drive to give it my all. It stayed with me through the years and was with me when I was training to swim the English Channel. I would hear his voice – 'Hang in there and don't give up!' – and it helped when I felt like I was freezing to death, with everything hurting and my brain desperately wanting to give up.

Swimming actually took a bit of a back seat during my childhood. For a while I preferred more popular sports such as cricket and rugby, as well as athletics.

At the age of eleven I went to public school, Trent College in Long Eaton, Nottinghamshire. It was thirty minutes from our house. My brother Mark was also a student there, although he was seven years older than me and in his final year just as I started. The school had fantastic facilities; it was perfect for someone like me, who loved sport. It had rugby and cricket pitches as well as an indoor swimming pool.

Rugby was the chosen sport at my school as they didn't play football, although I joined the Dayncourt FC Under-11s, based in our local village, Radcliffe-on-Trent. I remember proudly being top scorer in my first year, 1988.

In my first term at the school, I broke the 200- and 800-metre running records for my age group. By the time I turned twelve I was involved in rugby, cricket, athletics and rifle shooting. Unfortunately they later banned me from rifle shooting for firing at the target before the teacher told me to, saying I could have killed someone. I personally don't think it was my fault as one of the other kids shot before me, which prompted me to shoot, so I blame him. I also played cricket and rugby outside of school; as a cricketer I represented Derbyshire Under-13s at county level and was vice-captain for Derbyshire schools, as well as playing mini rugby for Nottingham Rugby Club in the winter.

Looking back, I was doing too much at this age, and not only all these sporting activities – I was also in the Boys' Brigade, which is like the Scouts. I didn't like it much; it wasn't my idea of fun, marching through the village playing the bugle very badly. I had to quit something. It ended up being swimming, football and Boys' Brigade.

By the age of thirteen I was playing sport all the time. I couldn't wait to get on the field. I would be looking at the time and gazing out of the window in school lessons, dreaming of being out there. I wasn't passionate about too many other school subjects that weren't sports-related. I did like English language and literature but it wasn't quite the same. My sports prospects seemed promising at this age, and it was always my dream to play professionally.

I started playing in the same village men's cricket team as Mark, who by now was twenty. He had my back on the field if anyone should upset me.

We had disagreements like all brothers, but Mark has always been supportive of me – not only on the pitch but in general throughout my whole life. My mum recalls a day when I was less than a year old and a lady took me down to the local village in my pram for a walk. Mark didn't trust her so he followed on his bike to make sure I was OK. (He was only six or seven at the time.) He got her into trouble by reporting back to my mum that the lady had lifted the fly net up because someone wanted to have a look at me. Even years later, when I was eighteen and at university, I forgot to ring him one evening as promised and he was so worried that he drove an hour to the campus to make sure I was OK.

At the age of thirteen, on one of my athletics training sessions, things took a turn for the worse. I received a bad injury to my right knee as I was jumping over hurdles and broke off some cartilage. I had an operation, but in those days keyhole surgery wasn't as sophisticated as it is now: the surgery was more invasive and the recovery time was longer. The operation involved cutting out the dead bone, which created a big scar on my knee. After a few months I was back swimming, although it put a halt to any more athletics, as my knee was never the same again. I also couldn't do rugby or contact sports for a while and when I did come back I never really recovered my form. Eventually I had to give it up to just play cricket and swim.

Swimming at school wasn't very popular. It seemed to be for people who didn't like sport but were forced to do some physical activity. The school had a small 25-yard pool and only very rarely would you find anyone using it. Competitions with other schools were few and far between and no one seemed to care even if you did win; it was hard to stand out in a sport that was not really given any credibility or taken seriously.

The pool was supervised by a man in his eighties affectionately known as Sarg. Even though he was a man of discipline, there was no real expectation for you to turn up to these sessions. There was no training programme and we were left to our own devices.

I would train every now and then, though when I say 'train' I use the word loosely, as it would normally involve floating around for most of the session and then psyching myself up to see if I could break the school's 50-yard backstroke record. The record was proudly displayed on a board by the pool and was held by a boy called Skelton. I didn't know him: he was my brother's age and it had stood for a number of years. Each time I went to the pool I would try to break it. Unfortunately, it never happened whilst I was at the school and it wasn't until I had left and was invited back to compete for the 'old boys' versus the current students that I did beat it, by over half a second.

At sixteen I enrolled into South Nottingham College of Further Education. I had made the decision to leave school as I wanted to study a subject that I was really passionate about, sport and leisure. The closest subject to this at college was a GNVQ/BTEC in leisure and tourism, which offered a similar level of qualification to A levels. The course was suited to me as a good part of it was practical, and I thought if I couldn't make it as a professional sportsperson then a job in the leisure industry might be the next best thing.

I didn't know what I was going to do as a career; there are so few jobs in sport and you have to excel at a top level to even be considered as a paid professional. Having suffered a bad injury so young didn't bode well for a career in sport but I still believed it was possible. That was until I participated in a football-coaching course at college and was involved in a tackle that resulted in the dislocation of my left knee. I was on my way to hospital in an ambulance when the knee popped back into place. Unfortunately the damage had already been done and I had to wear a cast for the next six weeks.

I was devastated, having just re-joined Bingham Swimming Club, and I was also still playing cricket for Radcliffe-on-Trent. It seemed so unfair that, yet again, I wouldn't be able to do the things I loved most in the world. I knew I would be really frustrated at not being able to play sport for another few months due to my knee being in a cast, so I decided to buy a waterproof plastic cover, which looked like a giant condom. It meant I could at least swim and shower. (I'm sure it was only meant for showers but I found I could swim OK and even do the odd tumble turn at the end of the pool.)

After six weeks the cast came off and, even though it was a while before I could play cricket, I didn't waste any time getting back into the pool and competing in swimming galas. A few months later I decided to compete at the Nottinghamshire County Championships, at which people with the best times in the county race against each other. I didn't know whether I would stand a chance, particularly as my knee had not long recovered and I hadn't done much training (not that I ever did much training anyway). I still went as my times had been quick enough in the 50-metre backstroke prior to the injury.

I remember that waiting to race was quite stressful. I did my heat and managed to qualify for the final. I was so surprised as I couldn't kick well at all with my knee; it affected my start underwater and on the turn. If you can't do a butterfly kick underwater then you have little chance of winning, as you are faster underwater than on top.

Before the final I was again very nervous. I sat in the changing room by myself, trying to stay calm until I received the call to walk down to our lanes. I took my lane and tried to motivate myself. I knew there were slightly faster swimmers in the heat but I had a chance.

The whistle blew for all the finalists to enter the water. My heart was pounding. Then: 'Take your marks . . . Go!' I threw my arms back, just two weak kicks underwater as the knee wouldn't allow more, and shot up to the surface before anyone else. I started winding my arms over as fast as I could. I always relied on power and believed that this made me go faster, although I have now learned otherwise. There were no rules at the time as to how far you could swim underwater. Since then, a ruling by FINA – the international governing body of swimming – has decreed that only 15 metres are permissible or you will face disqualification. But on this particular day, some of my competitors were going the majority of the length underwater and I didn't have a chance without a good leg kick. By the time my competitors surfaced I was towards the back of the pack. But I managed to fight my way into the field and turn with the leaders after the first length. My tumble turn was also very bad, though, and as I flipped my legs over it was a disaster. I was too far away from the wall and I pushed off with my right leg only, shooting straight up to the surface. I went from first to last in a couple of seconds. I tried to come back at the other swimmers, but it was too late. I managed to get to fifth place out of six.

It became very evident to me that the knee would only ever get me so far. I was as fast as anyone in the county on top of the water, but without a reasonable leg kick for starts and turns I knew I would never be able to reach the highest level necessary for professional competition.

After the championships, I found that having a girlfriend

and going out seemed much better pastimes than swimming. I was still a member of the club but didn't do much swimming for the next two years.

I came back to it at the age of nineteen for a brief stint. Swimming was more of a social thing to me by then, and I never put in the training and dedication required to take it to the next level. I knew I could still win my event, the 50-metre backstroke, at local and regional galas, and was happy with that due to my interest in other sports.

I really enjoyed my two years at college as I had the opportunity to play sport as well as study subjects I was interested in. I also liked the people; as it was further education, some of the students were a little older and more mature, and there was none of the hierarchy battling I had experienced in my school years.

At eighteen I went to the University of Wolverhampton, which I chose because it offered the subject I wanted, sports studies and leisure recreation management. (Also it wasn't too far from home to see my girlfriend.) I enjoyed most of university life and learned a lot – notably, thanks to my best friend Chris, how to get an extension in coursework and create more time for yourself.

2

SEARCHING FOR THE RIGHT PATH

In 1999 I left university and decided to travel to Australia to see my brother Kevin, who had emigrated over there. I had promised him I would visit after I finished my degree. It was in Australia that I met my wife. She came back to live in England with me and we moved in with my parents. I was twenty-one and still didn't have any idea of the career path I would take.

I came very close to becoming a PE teacher, but it would have meant another year at university and more debt. I wanted to earn some money and have my own independence.

I started looking at sales jobs. It was the natural thing for me to do as my dad and three brothers, Gary, Kevin and Mark, were all in this line of work. My dad had worked for Mars, the confectionary company, for twenty-seven years and I felt familiar with the sales environment.

It took around four months of searching to get a job. I knew it would be difficult with no previous sales experience, but

11

my dad had emphasised the importance of getting a good first job with a respected company, as it would set me up for a successful career path. I had an interview with Coca-Cola, landed the job and I was assigned a local patch to work. I was so happy and excited, and the job even came with a bright-red Coca-Cola van, so I had my own wheels. It also meant we could move out of my parents' place and buy our own house.

I moved to Nestle and then Butchers Pet Care, which were both steps up in my sales career. I had been at Butchers for two and a half years when my friend Mike mentioned that there was a position available where he worked, a small domestic-appliance manufacturer now known as Russell Hobbs. I thought this would give me useful experience in the non-food industry so I went for an interview and was offered the job.

I was twenty-six years old and had made yet another positive move in my sales career, but I knew there was still something missing from my life. I was bouncing from job to job, convincing myself that each move was a step towards my ultimate goal of becoming a sales director by the time I was thirty-five. But I wondered deep down whether this was what I really wanted or whether it was just a challenge I'd set myself for the wrong reasons.

Sport was still my true passion and I even applied a few times to work for sportswear and sporting-goods companies, just to get close to it.

The reality was that there was no chance now of achieving my dream of a sports career – it was too late and my body had too many injuries. No matter how much I wanted to be an athlete, it could never happen.

I hated to think of myself as a person who would tell his grandchildren, 'I could have been a professional cricketer or swimmer if things had worked out differently . . .', dwelling on my run of injuries and my failed attempt at a sporting career. And yet I often felt I didn't really belong in the world of business either. It was sport that dominated my mind; it had never left me since my school days. For a long time I endeavoured to channel this passion into my sales roles, and I worked really hard at achieving my targets with the same drive and tenacity that I knew from the sporting arena.

3

MY LIFE CHANGED IN AN INSTANT

In March 2006, I had been working for Russell Hobbs for over a year when I was again heading out to Australia for a holiday. During the flight, I had already watched two or three movies to fill the time and I was running out of entertainment options. I looked under the sport category and found a film called *On a Clear Day*. I hadn't a clue what the movie was about and the title certainly didn't give it away. It didn't sound particularly interesting until I read the description and discovered the film was about a man determined to salvage his self-esteem and tackle his demons by attempting the ultimate test of endurance: to swim the English Channel.

My situation wasn't exactly the same and yet I felt there were certain similarities between me and this character, Frank. For instance, I felt a little lost in my work life; I had recently given up cricket, a sport I had played all my life; I no longer swam competitively; and it seemed I had nothing much to strive for and look forward to. Watching Frank going through turmoil, lost and looking for something to break the cycle and give him focus, I was engrossed.

There is a part in the movie where Frank is on a ferry to France with his friends and he looks out to sea from the deck and says, 'How mad would you have to be to swim this?' His friends respond, 'Totally!' I got a huge shiver down my spine and knew in that moment that this was something I had to do. It was a fictional story about a fictional character, but it inspired me and I couldn't get it out of my head.

In life there are many ideas and thoughts that pass through our minds every day which are very quickly dismissed as unachievable. We convince ourselves that we are too old, too slow, not clever enough, not good enough, or that we don't have enough money or time. We are all guilty of it, finding many reasons why an idea or dream couldn't and shouldn't happen. Sometimes we seriously consider a new possibility only to be faced with others trying to knock it down, or with people who are so negative that we end up talking ourselves out of it.

When I made up my mind to swim the English Channel, I told very few people – not even my mum, who I thought would try to change my mind.

I had left the swim club eight years earlier, and even then I had swum mostly backstroke with the occasional one-length relay. I could only recall one occasion when I'd done front crawl non-stop for an hour, and that was when I was twelve years old. The closest I came to swimming now was to tread water in goal for my local water polo team, Southwell.

I didn't know anything about what it took to swim the English Channel. What training would be involved, the fitness required, and whether I was capable of swimming in very cold temperatures for hours on end. But for once in my life, I didn't care about these things. I became excited about the idea of it and didn't allow my brain to compute the negatives and evaluate my prospects. If I had analysed it in any depth, I'm sure I would quickly have convinced myself that the odds were stacked against me and it was simply not possible. I didn't allow that to happen. It was as if a light bulb had come on in my brain – I was convinced that this is what I was supposed to do.

My decision to give up cricket had been a difficult one, but it just wasn't worth keeping it up in the end – I was having two physio sessions a week on my knees just to play on a Saturday. This left a gap in my life which I needed to fill; maybe swimming the Channel was my calling, and the focus that I, like Frank, needed to give me direction and a purpose I felt I badly needed.

Very quickly after arriving in Australia, I started to research how to go about swimming the English Channel. I found out that approximately 1,000 people had swum it since 1875, when Captain Matthew Webb was the first man to do so. It is 21 miles at its narrowest point, between Dover and Cap Gris Nez. There are certain rules you have to adhere to for the swim to be official, which are based on how Captain Webb completed it. For instance, you can only wear a simple latex or silicon swim hat – not neoprene, as it is classed as too warm. No wetsuits are allowed, just standard swimwear, so trunks or shorts (which have to be above the knee) for the guys and a classic-shaped swimming costume for the ladies. You are not allowed to touch the support boat. You can drink and eat, but this has to be passed or thrown to you in a drinks bottle tied to a piece of string.

The cost for me would be £2,150. This would include admin fees and an observer on the support boat to officiate my swim and make sure I abided by the rules above – notably the one about not touching the boat at all during the crossing.

As well as solo attempts across the Channel, there are also relays in which each team member swims for one hour and then is replaced by another. Teams can vary in size from two people upwards. Crossing the Channel is seen as the Everest of swimming, although three times as many people have climbed Everest than have swum the English Channel. Those who want to conquer it do so for a number of reasons: some to raise money for a charity, some because it's a lifetime dream, and some, like me, who just want to see how capable they are.

I learned that swimmers have a choice of boat pilots who are officially approved for Channel attempts and that there are two federations, the Channel Swimming & Piloting Federation and the Channel Swimming Association. I also read that the currents are very strong and the conditions unpredictable, meaning that you don't know what you will face on the day or how long it will take you. Hypothermia is a very real possibility, as are encounters with jellyfish.

After reading all of this, it would have been understandable if I'd ended the idea right then and there. This was no longer a movie script – it was all very real. But the more I read, the more I became excited about taking on this challenge. The training would start as soon as I got home.

4

WHERE ON EARTH DO I START?

Upon returning home, I got straight into my training. I wasn't a member of a club and I didn't have a coach, so I decided I'd start with a swim before work. I arrived when the pool opened at 7 a.m. and thought the best test of my abilities would be to see if I could swim for forty-five minutes non-stop, like I had when I was twelve. I hated long-distance swimming as a kid and anything over two lengths was too far for me. I think part of the reason why I was so keen to challenge myself with this sport was because it was something I didn't like and wasn't very good at.

I changed into my trunks, excited by the thought that this was the start of an exciting new adventure. I pushed off from the side with great expectation and started to swim front crawl. It seemed strange, swimming up and down with no real purpose other than to complete each length and tick it off. I enjoyed the discipline and challenge of seeing if I could keep going for forty-five minutes.

My stroke was not great. I swam twenty lengths, followed by another thirty, under the illusion that my fitness would still be there from my childhood days, which was definitely not the case. I also found that I was holding my breath until the last minute, breathing only when I was just about ready to pass out. There was no rhythm to my stroke. But I tried not to focus on the things I was doing wrong; the goal was to finish the time I had set myself. After all, this was just the start.

I managed to complete the forty-five minutes and achieve my first goal on this journey, even though I was shattered by the end of it and had to face the stiff reality that I was a world away from swimming 21 miles on the open seas. I also had some discomfort in my shoulder, which had been caused by a save I had made in water polo some months before. At the time I'd heard a very loud cracking noise and it hadn't been right since. I tried not to think about it as injuries had prevented me from playing so many sports I loved in the past. I just put it to the back of my mind.

I was happy that I had put my line in the sand, making a commitment to this goal, and I was motivated to press on. I went back to the pool the next day and did the same again. I soon progressed from four sessions a week to five, and also increased the duration of the swims to one hour. When I could swim that comfortably without stopping, I challenged myself to hit the same 100-metre split times for the whole hour. My next goal was to reduce the split time and then vary the sessions to include 200-metre sets as well as 100 metres. I then tried to reduce my rest time from twenty seconds to fifteen and then ten. I stuck to similar sessions to gain a clear indication that I was getting faster, which was a good motivational boost.

As I grew fitter over the coming months, I would include a

longer session at the weekend, a non-stop swim covering 5–6 kilometres, just to see how my body reacted to it. (I realised later on that this was more of a confidence booster than something that increased my fitness.)

After five or six months' training, I had progressed better than expected. I was regimented with my training, going four or five times a week, and my speed had improved by fifteen seconds per 100 metres. I was also only resting for five or ten seconds between 100-metre sets, so I would only allow my heart rate to recover slightly before I pushed off again.

One Saturday I decided that I would test how long I could keep swimming for. My intention was to swim for three hours, which would be the longest I had ever completed in the pool. My previous best was two hours, which I had sectioned into lots of 100–200-metre swims with a set turnaround time – this kept my mind engaged with short-term targets. I found that, if I didn't do this and instead saw it as a straight two hours, my mind would drift and I would easily lose focus, which in turn would affect my speed and my will to complete the session.

On the day of my three-hour attempt, I only took a small drinks bottle with me and no food. I didn't like stopping for drinks as I was pushing against the clock.

I started around 7 a.m., to make the most of the pool's allocated lane-swimming time.

The lifeguards had seen me coming most mornings and were now used to me doing one or two hours, so I didn't mention that I was planning to swim for longer. At 9 a.m. the pool went from lane-swimming to public, and so I swam close to the side to stay out of everyone's way.

Once I reached three hours, I thought about stopping, but convinced myself to do another thirty minutes. Once I had done that I said to myself, 'I may as well do four hours.' This went on every half an hour until I reached five hours and called it a day.

I was thrilled that I had swum for that long and I now really believed I had a chance of swimming the English Channel. I knew I still had a long way to go: for one thing, this was a pool heated to 29 degrees centigrade while the English Channel would be 15–16 degrees at best, and I also had no idea how I would fare in open water. I sensed it would be a big challenge to get used to the cold.

The five-hour swim gave me a lot of confidence so I thought it was time to commit fully to the swim and pay the £1,000 deposit to reserve my boat. I looked online and decided to book the pilot who at that time had the most experience in taking Channel swimmers across, Mike Oram. I was so excited to book my slot – it was now official, which made me feel so much better. At times during my early training I had felt a bit of a fraud as I hadn't actually booked anything; I would ask myself, 'Are you really going to do it?'

I don't think I ever really doubted I would eventually book the swim, but I'd wanted to get to a point in my training when I felt confident enough in my own ability. It was still a very bold move as I hadn't even been in cold water yet. But I now believed I would do whatever it took to acclimatise to it. I'd wanted a new focus in my life and now I had it. This swim meant everything to me. It was also a great opportunity to raise money for two worthwhile causes: the Make a Wish Foundation, which grants magical wishes to young people with life-threatening conditions, and the cat rehoming centre from where I got my two cats.

My Channel crossing was booked for 10 July 2008 so I

had seventeen months to prepare. (I had tried for 9 July, my thirtieth birthday, but there wasn't a slot available then.) This was the second slot Mike had available on that tide as someone else had booked the first one. Some pilots can book up to four people on a week's tide – if one drops out the next person will get first choice of their slot and so on. Things can get moved around depending on the weather and the pilot will normally do his best to accommodate you if there's a delay, depending on how busy he is.

I was now desperate to test my capability in cold water. Up to this point I hadn't had any advice; it was just self-discipline that had got me this far. I was advised to phone the oracle of Channel swimming, Freda Streeter, about my training outside. The 'Channel General', as she is known, has supported many open-water Channel-swimming aspirants over a thirty-year period and is more often than not found on the beach at Dover Harbour from May to September, shouting orders, military-style, to keep swimmers disciplined.

I contacted Freda in February and she told me to stay out of the open water and stick to the pool until May, when it would be warmer. In the UK, February is one of the worst months to test your capability outside as it is a cold winter period and the water temperature is in single figures. You would have to be a very experienced cold-water swimmer to go in then – or completely crazy.

5

TIME TO TEST THE WATER

I knew what Freda said made sense but I just wanted to try it. I phoned up the National Watersports Centre in Nottingham and asked if I could book four swims. The gentleman who was responsible for watersports said, 'We don't have anyone swimming in the lake – especially this time of year.' I explained it would all be OK, I was training to swim the English Channel, and I would have someone to watch out for me. I managed somehow to convince him and he allowed me to go ahead.

When I arrived for the first of my four swims, it was a cold morning with frost on the ground. I changed into my trunks and sleeveless wetsuit. I hadn't done any research into buying a wetsuit – I just went out and bought the thinnest and cheapest one I could find. Not really appropriate for winter swimming!

One of the employees at the clubhouse decided to test the temperature before I jumped in: it was 9.7 degrees, which didn't sound that cold to me. I knew that the English Channel would be 5–6 degrees warmer, so I thought, 'Great – if I can handle this then the English Channel will be a piece of cake.' I was excited to test my capability.

I slipped into the water and immediately began to gasp for air. My chest felt like it was being crushed by a ten-ton weight. I was hyperventilating and trying to breathe. I put my hand on my chest to help me focus on getting oxygen in, but it was no help at all. This was like nothing I had ever felt before – the shock to my system was a real wake-up call about the effect cold water can have on the body.

In those first moments I was in the water, my wife saw I was struggling and suggested, 'Maybe you should get out?' I didn't want my first experience of cold water to be a one-minute wonder or to get in the habit of quitting. So I brushed it off and said, 'Oh, no, I'll be OK. I just needed a minute to get my breath back.' This was a complete lie. All that was running through my mind was how I wasn't going to last long in this temperature, how terrible the experience was, and how badly-prepared and naive I had been. I hadn't even planned how long I would be in the water for. I genuinely thought I would just keep going until I couldn't take any more, like I did in the pool.

As a minimum my objective was to swim the length of the lake and back, which was 4 kilometres. Once I had composed myself, my breathing started to settle down, and after a minute or so I began to swim. I did so with my head up, as I struggled to put my face in the water. I attempted a couple of times in the first few minutes to immerse my face, but it was like solid ice. Imagine having the worst ice-cream headache in the world and you're close to the pain. It was 500 metres before I gradually became used to it and could actually swim front crawl with my head in the water. Once I managed to immerse my face it felt more manageable, and surprisingly I felt like I could tolerate it after all. I had a strange numb glowing feeling in my face and I realised I couldn't actually feel my feet.

It was extremely hard to focus on anything else apart from how cold I was. After 750 metres I heard a boat come alongside me. I can only think that the guys at the sports centre were thinking, 'Why have we let this madman in the water?'

When I saw the guy on the boat my first reaction was to joke with him. I said, 'It's lovely and warm in here – you should come in!' Joking seems to be a tactic I instinctively use to stem nerves or distract myself from anything negative. The guy in the boat didn't respond; he just followed alongside me. As I reached 1,000 metres I surprised myself at how well I was doing, even though I felt like I was swimming pretty much frozen stiff.

I was trying my best to embrace the challenge of getting across the 2,000-metre lake. The lake was marked so I could tick off the distance in my mind. Once I reached 1,500 metres there was something clearly wrong: I started to lose feeling in my arms – they felt like lead weights – and I struggled to move through the water as it felt like I was pulling myself through treacle. My fingers looked like claws (this is one of the early signs of hypothermia), I felt disorientated and strangely paranoid. My pace slowed right down and it was now a battle to finish the final 500 metres. I kept throwing one arm in front of the other with no real power, just trying to drag my way through the water as best I could. It seemed to take for ever. I finally reached 2,000 metres and stood up. Immediately I thought, 'I have to swim back.' And then: 'If I can only swim two thousand metres at this temperature, how on earth will I be able to swim twenty-one miles?'

I was anxious and asked my wife to throw me the drinks bottle that was filled with warm carbohydrate drink. I didn't hear a response back so I asked her again. It dawned on me that my mouth wasn't functioning very well – it felt frozen stiff and the words I was trying to form didn't make any sense. Even I couldn't make out what I was saying! I said, 'Forget it – I'll swim back.'

I was serious when I said it, but I stood still for a minute, contemplating my next move. My body didn't want to do what my brain was telling it to. The will to continue was there, even though it was very apparent I was in no state to do so. Fortunately my brain reminded me how much trouble I was in and I asked the guy in the boat if he could take me back. I'm not sure he could understand a word I was saying, but he soon realised what I wanted when I started scrambling back into the boat. Trying to talk to him on the way back I sounded drunk; I knew what I wanted to say but the sounds coming out of my mouth were nonsense. He must have radioed ahead to the club as there was a lady waiting for me with a towel as I stepped onto dry land. I was shaking uncontrollably and stumbling all over the place. I sensed the embarrassment of the situation and when I was taken inside I was told to sit down. The room was spinning and I remember again trying to joke the situation off. I was given a warm cup of tea, although I was shaking so much I couldn't hold it without spilling it. I kept throwing it over myself – which was quite nice, actually, as it was a bit of heat.

The lady said, 'You have hypothermia – but don't worry, it's not that bad.'

I sensed it probably was quite bad but tried to put it out of my mind. She guided me to a shower and I saw myself in the mirror – I looked like a walking corpse! My face was a yellow and grey colour, as if all the blood had been sucked out of me. There was another chap I hadn't seen before by the shower, and it was all a bit confusing until I realised he was trying to switch on the heating for the shower and he couldn't make it work. It seemed to be taking for ever to switch it on. In reality it was probably only thirty seconds, but I was desperate to get warm and it felt like a lifetime.

Once it was fixed, I stepped under the shower. A paramedic appeared and started asking me questions, such as my name and where I lived. I could remember my name, but I was struggling with my actual address. I knew my town but I really had to concentrate on the street and house number. I also kept asking for the shower temperature to be turned up, as it felt barely lukewarm. The paramedic wouldn't let me, due to the dangers of heating up too quickly and the pressure that would put on my heart.

After forty-five minutes in the shower he took my temperature: 34.9 degrees. Anything under 35 degrees and you are classed as hypothermic. As I started to warm up I could see blood patches across my chest as heat began to move back to my extremities. The paramedic said that if I had stayed in the cold water just another couple of minutes I would probably have gone under and that would have been it.

After around an hour, my core temperature had recovered to a normal 37 degrees and I was allowed to go home. I was told not to drive, though, so I cancelled a customer meeting the next day – an odd conversation in which I had to tell him I couldn't make it as I had hypothermia and had nearly died.

That evening I went to bed wearing a T-shirt and three thick fleeces to stay warm. I was concerned about going to sleep, for fear of not waking up.

I did fortunately wake up the next morning, to a huge reality check. I had been very lucky – I realised how serious my condition had been and how confused I had felt. I had underestimated the enormous effect extreme cold water can have on an inexperienced body that has not been acclimatised to it. The consequences could have been devastating.

At this point I would have been forgiven for giving up this crazy idea of swimming the English Channel. But my experience in the lake actually had the opposite effect: it made me more determined than ever. I thought, 'If I'm stupid enough to nearly kill myself over my lack of knowledge and experience of open water, I'd better put it right by doing it properly!'

After a couple of days out of the water, I went back in the pool. I had learned a dangerously harsh lesson – one I knew I would never forget. I didn't tell many people about what had happened, and in particular didn't share it with my parents as my mum didn't really understand what I was doing. (She is a worrier at the best of times – what she didn't know couldn't hurt her!) I was determined that this experience would make me stronger. I now knew what it felt like to have severe hypothermia.

6

IF AT FIRST YOU DON'T SUCCEED . . .

It wasn't until July 2007 that I went back into open water. I contacted Freda Streeter again to let her know I would be coming down to Dover, judiciously leaving out the details of my incident in February.

When I arrived, there was another first-timer there and Alison Streeter (Freda's daughter, who has swum the English Channel many times) was about to take her into the sea. She said I could go with them and I knew I couldn't be in better hands. That said, we hadn't discussed how long I was to swim with them for – I think the plan was to swim to the harbour wall and back, so thirty minutes at the most, I guessed.

I was a little nervous entering the water, as the vivid memories of my February swim came creeping into my mind. I ventured out with them anyway and swam right to the harbour wall. As I turned back I realised I had managed to lose them both, so I just carried on swimming back and forth to each harbour wall for the next few hours. I thought Alison would probably be looking for me or trying to get my attention, but when I looked back I couldn't see anyone.

At this point I didn't know what the protocol was – whether to keep swimming or come in. We'd only planned to do a short dip, but the competitive side of me took over. I just kept swimming, wanting to test how long I could swim this comfortably. I went for one hour, then two. At three hours I started to think someone might be worried about me, and at three and a half I was getting quite hungry. I didn't know whether it would be good for me to continue without food or drink and I didn't want them sending the water police after me. As I walked back onto the beach I heard someone shout, 'We wondered when you were going to come in!' This was Barry, one of the volunteers at Dover; he returns every year to help out with food and drink, or appears with plastic gloves to rub Vaseline under your arms and neck. Like a lot of supporters on the beach, he gives his time unconditionally and this support really does make all the difference to the swimmers.

This swim had put me back on track and it was still only my second time in open water. It gave me the boost I needed, helping me to rebuild my confidence and put the demons from the last swim to bed.

Driving the long journey home I felt euphoric and was already thinking about how I might improve for my next swim the following weekend. At this point I was swimming in the pool five or six times a week, before and after work, whenever I could fit it in.

I was going home with a real sense of self-belief. Although I still hadn't swum the qualifier of six hours (which as part of the rules needs to be completed in order for you to be allowed to swim the Channel), I felt that my training was all heading in the right direction. It was strange to think that, since taking up this challenge, and at every stage, I had always believed I had a chance of succeeding. I would tell myself, 'It's just one arm in front of the other – keep it simple.' I wished I had thought that way in cricket, instead of allowing the fear of failure to hold me back. By focusing on negative scenarios like losing my wicket, I lost the ability to play to my natural game. At practice in the nets I would hit the ball fluently and not even think about it, but out in the middle of the pitch I'd find that my feet wouldn't move the same way and I would be tight and stiff, playing consciously rather than subconsciously. In other words I was overthinking it. The trouble was, the more I overthought it, the more my batting performance would suffer; even when I did do well I would criticise myself, thinking I could still have done better. And this way of thinking meant that I never relaxed, mentally or physically – it became a habit to think of myself in that way.

In open-water swimming I couldn't afford to think like this and worry. So much of my success rested on mental strength. I wish I had known then what I know now about the power of positive thought and the importance of not overthinking a performance.

I drove back to work bright and early the next day. Even before I started the swim training, it had always been a drag making the 190-mile round trip to work most days. This time felt particularly tiring, after my three-and-a-half-hour swim and seven-hour round trip to Dover. I was expected to be in the office every Monday and had no choice if I wanted to get paid, so I just had to get used to it.

As the week went on, I was looking forward to the next swim and wondered what I should try for. Maybe four hours, four and a half . . . That would be a natural next step. I had heard from the other swimmers that you are informed by Freda how long you are going to do and you don't get a say in it. No negotiation: you just do it. There is a reason for this military approach and it is not because she is trying to be mean. When the day of your crossing comes and you have to get on with it, you don't get to negotiate with the sea about how long you can swim that day or what sort of weather conditions you would like. You can only do your best to prepare for what may get thrown at you, and being afraid of Freda's wrath is a great incentive to stay in the water and do as you are told.

The weekend arrived and I made the long journey to Dover on the Saturday, leaving just after 5 a.m. I put my things on the beach along with all the other swimmers and gave my name so I could be registered.

Freda asked me when my Channel swim was booked for. I told her next July and she asked how long I had swum for the previous week. When I told her three and a half hours, she instantly replied, 'Try six hours.' Strangely that's what I wanted; I wanted to see if I was capable of ticking this landmark off. It was only my third proper open-water swim, but I knew the confidence it would give me to complete it.

I wandered into the water pumped up and focused for the job in hand. I didn't have time to overthink it, which was a good thing. There are a lot of things that can unsettle your mind; for instance, not only are you swimming in the cold sea, non-stop, for six hours . . . but you are doing so wearing just your swim trunks, goggles and swim cap. You cannot get out of the water and you try not to stand up or rest, as this would only be cheating yourself and would disqualify your swim on the real thing. After two hours you get a drink thrown to you, and again every sixty minutes after that. The feed should take a few seconds and then you just keep swimming.

The water felt more comfortable somehow. It was a similar temperature as the previous week, but I didn't have the same feeling of trepidation and I wasn't analysing it as I had last time. What I realised is that it's important to respect the sea, but give it too much respect and it will dominate you, making you question your capability and whether you're worthy to take it on.

I focused on how well I had done the week before and used that to give me the confidence I needed. I now knew I could swim for three and a half hours and I also knew I had had energy left in the tank, so there was no excuse not to do the same again – and more.

The first couple of hours were a little boring. It was a relief this time knowing that I would be able to get a drink along with the rest of the swimmers who were scheduled to do long sessions. The majority of open-water swimmers use a carbohydrate powdered drink that provides slow-release energy. At the beach they also provided a warmed cordial with no extra sugar, which is added for taste. I received mine on the second hour, in a plastic cup. I didn't like the taste but I could feel the liquid warming my insides, and although I didn't really want it, I could feel the benefit.

I drank it as fast as I could, as I wanted to get into the habit of practicing as if it were my actual swim. I carried on in the same direction as the majority of the swimmers, which is to go directly left towards the harbour wall and then, once you get close to the far end, you turn back and swim the full length in the opposite direction. It is around 1,400 metres from one harbour wall to the other. It took me about fifteen minutes from the drinks station to the left wall, and a further twenty or twenty-five minutes to the far right wall. I had decided to wear a watch so I knew how long I had been in for; I noticed that some of the others wore them and that those who didn't relied upon the big clock at the end of the harbour wall. The reason people do not wear them is to resist the temptation to keep looking and feel that time isn't passing very quickly. (On the actual Channel day, all swimmers are advised not to wear a watch.)

I realised, as I continued, that I was swimming faster in one direction than the other; at the time I convinced myself this was due to my speed, when in reality it was the wind and current.

Getting to the three-hour mark seemed tougher than before, and I wondered whether it was because I had swum three and a half hours the previous week and now had no incentive, or because I knew I was only halfway to six hours. It was probably a bit of both. I decided to focus on another short-term goal – swimming four hours – and thought, 'How great will I feel when I achieve it and pass my previous best?'

I passed three and a half hours and didn't feel quite the same buzz as the week before. I'm sure this was because I had known then that I was getting out and had surpassed expectation. It is amazing how much better you feel when you know you are finishing. When I knew I could stop whenever I wanted to, there was no particular pressure. I needed to learn to swim with this pressure so that I could understand how to handle it.

As I swam through the four-hour mark, I was expecting to feel elated. But instead of focusing on the achievement, I began to focus on how tired I felt, and how was I ever going to complete the Channel if I could only do four hours feeling the way I did. I kept telling myself, 'Just one more hour . . .' and, 'I'm on the final swim and in.' I tried different tactics to make the time go by. Thinking about work made me feel negative and notice the cold, and singing didn't relax me – I just seemed to lose concentration. I visualised my dad saying, 'Don't give up – give it everything you've got!', just as I had when I was a child competing in the pool. This helped drive me on.

As I reached the five-hour mark I felt instantly better, knowing I was on the final straight –the last hour. I came in for my last drink at around five hours ten minutes, giving myself just fifty minutes to finish. I knew that all I needed to do now was swim to the left harbour wall, then right and back to the beach to finish. No matter how hard I tried not to do it, I ended up looking at my watch every five minutes of that fifty-minute stretch, ticking them off.

As I made the final swim in, I felt goosebumps – and not from the temperature. It was from the realisation of what I had done: it was a major step in the right direction in accomplishing my dream of swimming the English Channel.

I walked up to the top of the beach feeling a little dizzy and cold, but I wasn't half as bad as I thought I would be. Freda said, 'Well done', and told me to get dressed quickly. Fortunately I had come prepared and had packed some emergency layers of clothing, including fleeces, tops and a woolly hat that I had purchased specially the week before. Freda told me to keep my swim hat on, dry it off and then put the woolly hat on top of it. I was desperate to take it off, not least because having latex stuck to your head for six hours is not the most comfortable form of headwear, but also because, by taking it off, I would be confirming to myself that the swim was over. I knew deep down it made complete sense to leave it on and keep the heat I had generated in; as I later found out, there is a theory that 80 per cent of your body heat is lost through your head.

I quickly got dressed. I was shaking vigorously but I didn't care. I was so happy to have completed the six-hour challenge, and on only my third open-water swim. Once I had all my layers on I was given a warm drink, which was greatly appreciated, and yet here was another challenge: how to drink it! It may sound like a basic task, but trust me, when you've been immersed for six hours in cold temperatures, it is a challenge in itself due to the excessive shaking of your body. You need superpowers of concentration to keep your hands still. The other issue is that a cup of tea at normal temperature – say, 80 degrees – feels volcanic until your core heats up, which can take some time. I made a mental note for future training that warm drinks should actually only be lukewarm so that you can drink them without the feeling of scalding yourself.

They were starting to pack up on the beach and there was talk of going to a local café, which the swimmers would often go to after a weekend training session. I thought I would go along and get some food in the system before travelling back – as I was starving. I felt I could eat an endless supply of food, and the sugar cravings were unbelievable. It was great to meet up with a bunch of like-minded individuals and I felt part of something special, like an elite club. I had been a part of other sports clubs before and yet this seemed different. There appeared to be no hidden agendas and everyone seemed to be very genuine and caring, with an appreciation of what you have to go through to succeed in this extreme sport. I wondered whether that was due to the fact that you are not competing with each other. The challenge is between you and nature, not against other individuals. It's not a race.

What I also liked was that those people who were slower swimmers were just as respected as the faster swimmers. Being slower means you have to endure the elements for longer; some people have swum for over twenty-five hours non-stop, battling Mother Nature.

I made my way back home after a good fill of food and drink. It wasn't ideal as I had already driven for hours in the morning, swum six, and was now having to drive back. I didn't have a choice, though, as I had work again in the morning. I spent the drive trying to stay awake – another challenge!

As soon as I arrived home, I collapsed on the couch and was incapacitated for the remainder of the night, trying not to think about the 95-mile drive early in the morning. I fell asleep on the sofa and had to pick myself up the next day and make the dreaded journey.

7

YOU GET OUT WHAT YOU PUT IN

It would be tough to go to Dover to train every week, so I knew I would have to balance it with pool training and find a more local place to swim in open water. Freda had told me after my Dover swim that there was a Channel relay team who were short a fourth swimmer for an attempt in August, and that two of the guys were from Nottingham – my home town. She said it would be a good opportunity for me to get a feel for what it would be like to swim the whole distance by myself as a solo.

It made a lot of sense and I wanted to prepare myself in the right way. So I contacted the organiser of the relay, who was a nice guy called Colin Bycroft. He had plans to swim a solo across the English Channel and had changed the attempt into a relay after suspecting he wasn't yet ready. I thought joining his team would be a good way of understanding what I was up against.

In many ways the relays are very similar to solo crossings, in terms of both what you are allowed to wear and the number of strict rules you have to observe. The main difference is that you swim for just one hour at a time, without touching the boat; the next swimmer must jump in behind you and swim past you, to ensure that all the distance is covered. The timing has to be spot-on too: one hour, no more and no less, before the next swimmer takes over. The maximum relay number to date is eight people, but six or fewer is more common. The boats used in Channel crossings tend to be used for fishing when they are not taking swimmers out, and so there is limited room, hence the restricted numbers. In addition, the more swimmers there are, the less each team member will have to swim; too many swimmers could take some of the challenge element away from it. The relay I was enquiring about was ideal for me as it was just four people and therefore it was likely I would get at least three swims at an hour each time, which would be perfect.

The rules are set and governed by the two swimming associations mentioned in Chapter 3. Both are very credible, with similar rules and registered pilots who have great knowledge and in-depth experience of taking swimmers across the Channel. For the swim to be official it must be through one of these organisations. Doing otherwise could be very dangerous – the rules and regulations are there for the swimmers' safety. Sadly, to date, there have been eight reported deaths of people trying to swim the English Channel. One of those tragedies was a British man who attempted to swim without a pilot boat and against official advice in 1954. His body was later found washed up in Holland.

I spoke to Colin and the relay space was still available so I committed straight away. I was really excited to see what it would be like – test the water, so to speak. We called the team

TACC as each initial represented a team member: Tony, Adam (me), Chris and Colin. Not the most inspirational name in the world, but it worked for us.

We didn't have a long time together before we were due to do the actual swim so we thought we'd better have a training session as a team. Three of us agreed to go to Dover on the regatta weekend in August, just two weeks before the Channel swim; unfortunately Colin couldn't make it.

We arrived after 9 a.m. Freda hated anyone being late as this sport is all about discipline. For a lady who was barely over five foot and approaching seventy years old, she certainly had a way of putting the wind up you.

I now felt really confident about my swimming, following my six-hour success a few weeks earlier, and for the first time I felt that I had earned the right to call myself an open-water swimmer.

The three of us waded into the water together and started swimming. We hadn't swum together before and were unsure of each other's speeds. It was nice for me to swim with other people, as nearly all my swimming had been done alone until this point.

Because relay swimming involves giving it your best for an hour at a time, the training and preparation are different than for a solo. After one hour, Tony decided to leave the water, get dry and come back in an hour later. After a short debate, Chris and I decided to keep going. We both wanted to maximise our time there and I had no excuse after my previous swims at Dover. True to his word, Tony joined in again an hour later. This is in fact good practice for relay swimmers – training as if you are on your actual relay swim – as it is not easy to get back in the water once you have warmed up.

During the second hour I suddenly felt a huge thud at the side of my temple, as if someone had shot me. My head slammed forward into the water and I had a small cut. I was completely confused as to what had just happened. Looking around, I couldn't see anything that I might have swum into – there was nothing around me. I then looked up at the road above and saw a group of sheepish-looking teenage kids. I stopped swimming and went over to them and shouted, 'Did one of you throw a stone?' They started laughing to themselves – 'No!' The biggest boy, who was around fifteen years old, stepped forward and said, 'It wasn't them – don't have a go at them!'

'If you want to be tough,' I said, 'why don't you come in here and tell me face to face?' I was so mad. They could have killed me.

I continued swimming to catch up with the others, who were unaware of what had happened. The incident had not only distracted me from my training but also really annoyed me, which isn't a good feeling when this sport is all about being relaxed. We turned around and I started swimming back to get out. As it was a regatta weekend with lots of events happening on the beach during the day, the police were around. I climbed out of the water and ran up the beach to advise Freda of what had just happened. She too was annoyed and immediately told someone on the beach to report them. By the time the police were notified, however, the kids had sensed what was happening and had run off. There was nothing I could do now. I was just thankful it wasn't more serious.

All in all, it wasn't quite the training session I had envisaged, but we still managed to complete some good distance.

We only had the chance to do this one session together as the relay was scheduled for 31 August. (There is no guarantee on dates with this sport, though, as it is very much dependant on the sea and weather conditions.) As excited as I was about the relay, I knew that my main focus was to swim across the Channel solo. But with ten months still to go until I attempted it, this would be a good test in preparation.

The three of us travelled down to Dover the evening before our Channel relay. We met up with Colin and the pilot, Eddie Spelling, at his 42-foot boat, *Anastasia*. It was the biggest of all the Channel-swimming boats, with lots of room for bags and plenty of upper-deck space, so visibility for supporting each other would be good.

It seemed we had all brought enough food and drink to last a week. The funny thing was that we had all received the same advice from people on what food and drink to take on the boat. We therefore brought multiples of Pot Noodles, Jelly Babies and Jaffa Cakes. (I would definitely recommend that relay teams discuss this beforehand and organise a checklist of food as well as other items, to avoid making the same mistake we did. Talk to your pilot about the facilities on the boat as well.)

We stepped onto the boat and met the crew. Eddie immediately started shaking his head, saying it wasn't looking good for a swim the following day, which changed the team's mood instantly. He said it was likely to be rough sea and asked the swimmers' capabilities. I was feeling confident to go whatever the weather, but this was no time to be macho and I had team members and safety to consider. I didn't want this to be a miserable and unsafe experience for them. We knew from training together that Chris and Tony were good swimmers, but as we hadn't had a chance to swim with Colin, we were unsure of his ability beyond his own assessment that he was slow.

I had heard from other Channel swimmers that weather conditions can be a real issue, with some having to postpone their attempt until the following year if their agreed swim date came and went and the pilot had no alternative slots available. I was concerned this might be the situation with us. There was nothing we could do now, however; it was a case of assessing the conditions in the morning.

Open-water Channel swimming season starts at the end of June and runs until the end of September. This is mainly due to the temperature of the water before and after those dates, when it normally drops below 15 degrees and is too cold to swim in for any length of time. Having said this, the average temperature for the North Channel in the summer months is actually 13 degrees or less.

There are now groups of swimmers who swim through the winter months. These hardy individuals, also known as ice swimmers, challenge themselves to swim a mile in under 5 degrees, without a wetsuit. There are race events held all around the world for this new test of survival, and there is even now a World Winter Swimming Championships. Who knows – maybe in the future it will be part of the Olympics?

Back in Dover, we spoke to Eddie the next morning and his thoughts were the same as the previous evening: the conditions could be quite poor. We collectively felt like a strong team so we all made the decision to do the swim. If one person hadn't agreed we wouldn't have gone – everyone had to be willing.

8

A TASTE OF
THINGS TO COME

We brought all our gear to the boat (including our ridiculous amounts of Pot Noodles and Jaffa Cakes) and off we went to Shakespeare Beach in Dover, which is one of the starting points when swimming the English Channel. Eddie stopped the boat 75 metres from the beach – as close to the land as he dared go without being grounded.

We had previously agreed that the swimming order would be based on speed, from quickest to slowest. This meant that I would start, which was a real honour. I would have a taste of what it would be like at the start of my solo swim. Our relay wouldn't officially commence, however, until I was standing on the beach at Dover. (These rules can vary from channel to channel depending on whether it is possible to leave the water; if not, the swimmer needs to touch a rock near the land to start.)

I jumped in and swam the short distance to the beach. I did a pretend celebration as I cleared the water, for a joke and to relax myself. I couldn't believe that I was standing in Dover, about to swim across the English Channel with a group of guys I hardly knew. I felt nervous – but the good nerves you get from a lot of excitement with a little apprehension.

For the first time in a long while, I felt a sense of purpose. I know that, to many people, swimming across a body of water between one piece of land and another may not sound like it has a point. But to me it felt like I was doing something uniquely challenging, and it gave me some direction. At that time, everyday life wasn't giving me what I needed; I had spent many years frustrated with my career and not knowing why. I knew deep down that there was something not right – that this wasn't how I was supposed to live my life. Don't get me wrong: I hadn't had a bad life. I just didn't feel completely fulfilled. It was not until this very moment that I found what I was looking for.

I stood on the beach and waited for a signal. A horn was sounded to signify the start of the swim and off I went. I had so much adrenaline that I dived into the water as if it were a 50-metre Olympic race. I felt all eyes on me and wanted to give it everything I had; I didn't want to let my team down. My heart was pounding but I was also very excited. The waves were choppy, which added to the challenge.

We had brought with us two laminated sheets, one with the number 30 on it and one with the number 5. These were a great asset to the team, as they indicated to the swimmer the number of minutes left before changeover. My own first hour seemed to take no time at all and then it was Chris's turn to enter the water. Tony was waiting with a towel and my clothes to help dry me off.

We fell into a nice routine of one team member helping the person who had just finished and climbed out of the water, while the other team members watched the current swimmer and cheered him on. One after another we completed our hours. You have to keep to the same order you are given by the observer at the start: it cannot be changed, no matter what happens. Even if one of you is suffering from seasickness or cramp, for the swim to count each person has to do their full hour without touching the boat before the next one jumps in.

We all agreed to swim on the left side of the boat, trying to keep towards the middle section. We chose not to switch sides as this would lose us time and potentially cause confusion.

At one stage Colin started to swim off course and we all wondered whether he wanted to make a detour to Belgium. The boat had to sound its horn a few times to bring him back, which made us laugh. In fairness, though, he wasn't as experienced a swimmer as the rest of us, but he gave it his all.

The water temperature was around 16 degrees, which felt very manageable to me as I was confident from completing my six-hour swim in a similar temperature only a few weeks before, and I knew I could comfortably tolerate it for one hour at a time.

The hours seemed to pass much faster than expected. Soon the three-hour mark ticked by, the others had successfully completed their one-hour swims, and I was in again. The toughest part was getting out, becoming warm, and then having to strip off into your trunks and do it all again.

My second swim was similar to the first, although my shoulder was a little more painful this time. The shoulder had gradually become worse over the past few months through training, and my increased mileage was taking its toll. I tried to adjust my swim stroke to avoid catching my shoulder, but I found I was pulling across the middle of my body, affecting my speed and efficiency. I was also potentially damaging my shoulder and was concerned that I may not be able to do the solo if I carried on with this technique.

We were all going very well and the transitions between swimmers went like clockwork. Colin appeared to feel the cold a little more than the rest of us when he climbed out of the water. We all enjoyed a hot drink during our time on the boat. I have never been a huge fan of hot drinks, but when you climb out of the water in this sport, it's the equivalent of being out in the desert, dying of thirst, and finally finding a bottle of ice-cold water. The warm liquid instantly gives you a feeling of internal insulation – like being defrosted from the inside out.

Everything seemed to be going according to plan and even though the conditions were rough we were making good headway. By the time I started the third swim it was getting dark. Although we looked close to France, looks were deceptive and we were still a few miles from land. It wasn't until Colin was back in swimming three hours later that I sensed we were near finishing, as I could see a huge dark shadow of land in the near distance. It was now pitch-black, and although there was a light on the side of the boat, it would blind the swimmer whenever he turned to breathe. We decided to shine a torch on the surface of the water just ahead of each team member, as it was disorientating trying to work out where to go.

I was convinced Colin would finish the swim, which would

have been a fitting way to complete our relay as it was he who had formed the team. But fifty minutes into his final swim, it became apparent that this wouldn't be the case – I would need to go in for a fourth time. I had wrapped myself up warm and was fully clothed, not expecting to go in again, so although I wasn't bursting to jump back in, I knew what a great honour it would be to finish the relay for the team.

When I jumped in we were still over a mile away. I treated it as a one-mile training session and started to sprint as soon as I hit the water. It was really exciting, although I was struggling to see as I felt blinded by the light whenever I turned towards the boat. I tried to breathe to the other side but this resulted in me zigzagging all over the place.

After fifteen minutes or so I could see one of Eddie's boat crew starting to release a RIB into the water in preparation for the finish. I kept looking behind me, waiting for him to appear, which seemed to take ages. I realised this wasn't doing me any good, so I switched back to the job in hand and ignored what was going on behind me.

After another twenty minutes or so, the boat appeared alongside me and the man inside shouted, 'Follow me.' I did just that, although it was quite choppy and I felt myself getting caught in a rip current. I looked up after thirty seconds and couldn't see him very well; after another thirty seconds he'd moved again. It was all very confusing and I thought I wouldn't like to have this in a channel solo after swimming all day.

Finally he came alongside me again and said, 'There is a rock in front of you – go and touch it and swim back.'

Normally you clear the water in an English Channel swim,

but he was concerned about the dangers as he only had a small torch and I didn't have any visibility. I couldn't see a thing as it was so dark but he told me that it was around 25 metres away.

I started swimming towards what I thought was straight ahead. I even tested myself by closing my eyes and opening them again, but it didn't seem to make a difference to my visibility in the black of the night. I couldn't even see my hand going into the water, and with every stroke I felt for rock. After a very tentative 25 metres or so, I finally felt something jagged and solid.

I shouted, 'I've touched it!'

He replied, 'Come back!'

But even though I thought I had touched the rock I started to question myself and feel around for other rocks to touch, to make 100 per cent sure I had actually reached land. I wanted to be certain that I finished properly.

I started to swim back in the darkness and was again quite tentative as I still couldn't see anything. After a minute or so, I saw the torchlight flashing from the RIB. I wondered whether I would see the others jumping in to join me, but this wasn't the case, for safety reasons. The RIB took me back to the boat and everyone was waiting and cheering each other. We had done it – we had swum the English Channel as a team! Chris broke out the champagne and we celebrated our feat.

It had been a privilege to swim with these guys and I had gained some good friends out of it too. There had been a risk that swimming in a relay would have an adverse effect on me, create self-doubt – it was my first real understanding of how much it would take to swim solo from England to France. I knew I couldn't compare a relay to swimming it all myself, but it was a big step forward towards achieving my dream. It made me hungrier than ever!

9

IT WAS NEVER
GOING TO BE EASY

I found it hard going back to work following such a high. I felt so happy, with a real sense of achievement, and I couldn't wait to get back in the water and train.

The relay would be the last time I went into open water until April the following year – the year of my solo attempt. There was no loss of focus in the pool, though, and I was very quickly back into my five or six sessions a week. I wanted to make sure no stone was left unturned and to be as prepared as possible. My life from now on would revolve around when I could train; it became a constant focus. The swimming became a priority over my job and most other things in my life, which didn't make life easy. If I was going to be self-disciplined, sacrifices had to be made.

I had to be in the office a minimum of three days a week and there was an expectation that I would have meetings on the other two days. I found myself constantly thinking about how I could create more time for training, which had become as much a part of my daily routine as eating and sleeping. I craved it and couldn't get enough, even feeling guilty if I didn't do something each day – but in the back of my mind was always the concern over my shoulder and how much of this it could take. I felt tired a lot of the time due to all the driving and trying to balance things, but I realised that if you want something enough you will create the time to do it.

I knew the swimming pool's timetable off by heart, and when working from home I would head over there for the hour-long adult lane-swimming slot around lunchtime. Sometimes I would even sneak off while supposedly working at home, phoning my boss from the leisure centre car park, just before I went into the pool, knowing he was less likely to want to speak to me again in the next hour if we had just had a conversation. Many times I would run to my locker after a session to check my phone, praying that he hadn't called. More often than not I would get away with it; on other occasions I would make up some excuse, like I'd been on the other line to a customer. I thought, 'As long as I do the work and achieve results, what he doesn't know can't hurt him – or me.'

I mostly did pool work and where possible integrated a couple of gym sessions a week. The reality was that, unless it was the weekend, I would struggle to do both. My gym work normally consisted of an hour and a half of mixed cardio on the exercise bike or cross trainer, then arms, shoulders and back. I didn't do too much chest work as I was regularly working my chest in my swimming and I was conscious of being too dominant in that area. I would lift lighter weights and do four sets of fifteen to twenty reps, on average, to build muscular endurance.

I was still driven to succeed in my work, even though my current role had become less meaningful. I felt the Channel swim represented something much bigger and more important than my normal day-to-day job. I had always felt I was capable of something memorable in my life, and after the disappointment of so many injuries, this was a way of overcoming adversity. I realised the water was where I belonged. I'd had such a strong affinity to it all my life, yet never given it my full attention until now. I wanted to show myself I could really excel at something I cared about.

At the same time I was creeping towards the age of thirty and wanted to put some markers down in my life, to have something to really strive for. My job just didn't do that for me. I admired those who were passionate about their work, but no matter how much I pushed to achieve this for myself, I just couldn't seem to get the same sense of fulfilment.

When I first went into sales, I remember my dad saying, 'My concern for you is how sensitive you are and how much you may take things to heart.' My dad was right – the sales world is not one for sensitive people. I am the type of person who likes to get on with everyone, I like building relationships with people, I don't like letting anyone down, and I care far too much for my own good. I found that I would become easily stressed if buyers shouted at me about quality issues or our products being late for delivery, a lot of which was out of my control but I would take it personally all the same. I would try to remind myself that I wasn't trying to resolve world peace or famine – I was selling a kettle or a can of pet food. My mum jokingly used to say to me, 'Well, you just don't like work. I think you would get sick of any job.' I was worried she might be right.

Throughout the winter, my shoulder continued to hurt. I saw a physiotherapist as regularly as I could, to try to relieve the pain. Although this made it easier for a short period of time, I knew there was something wrong which couldn't be manipulated out or released. The pain was constant. As the months went by and training increased, I grew more concerned that the shoulder could tear at any point. I would focus on it all the time – it became like a protective mechanism in my mind, almost as if I was gearing up for an excuse if I didn't make it. It is human nature to protect ourselves from disappointment

My physio's name was Teresa Dixon. She had treated me in the latter stages of my cricketing days, when my knee would swell up like a balloon and I needed up to two physiotherapy sessions a week just to get back on the pitch. Teresa knew I was becoming more anxious about the shoulder and she recommended a friend of hers who worked at the clinic doing hypnotherapy, as she thought it would help my mental focus.

I have to confess, I didn't know much about hypnotherapy, I thought it involved someone swinging a pendulum back and forth while they brainwashed you into thinking you were a chicken or made you bark like a dog. I was sceptical because I didn't understand it, but I was willing to try anything that might help.

The hypnotherapist's name was Clem Turner. I arranged to have a session with him at his home studio and he greeted me like a family member he hadn't seen for years. Instantly I liked him and felt at ease. He is one of those people who you just warm to straight away, and I could sense he really cared about his patients.

I sat down in his very comfortable leather chair and he took a few personal details and asked me about my issue. I explained it was about my shoulder and how worried I was that it would affect me swimming the English Channel. After listening to my concerns, he passed me some headphones and told me to close my eyes and relax. He then proceeded to talk to me through the headphones, initially getting me into a state of hypnotic relaxation. I had never done anything like this before and wanted to laugh. Not because he was saying anything funny; I just developed the giggles.

I am not great at shutting off mentally, so trying to completely relax my brain was a new experience for me. The technique he used is very clever, putting you into a state of relaxation which then makes you open to suggestion. I went into more detail about my shoulder concerns, and once I was relaxed he integrated positive thoughts to take my mind away from the pain.

When the session finished, Clem asked me how long I thought I had been there for.

'About five minutes?' I guessed.

'It's actually been forty-five minutes,' he replied.

I couldn't believe it – the time had flown by. I felt relaxed and revitalised. I couldn't believe how effective the session had been – it was as if I had been given an injection of positivity. I thought to myself, 'This stuff really works!'

I left Clem's house with a spring in my step. It had been great to switch off for that short period of time and just listen to his voice shutting out all the perils of daily life. He also gave me a CD that would help me relax and bring back the feelings I had had in the session.

I had never before stopped to really think about the

importance of my mindset and how what I focused on could determine my outcome. There was a realisation I would have to train my brain as well as my body if I wanted to succeed.

10

STATE
OF MIND

I booked a distance-swim camp in Gozo, Malta, at the start of the new open-water season in April 2008. It was the ideal location for Channel training as the water temperature would be very similar, and it would also allow me to get another six-hour swim under my belt. I knew if I could get one completed early it would be a great confidence boost before my solo Channel swim later in the season.

I had managed to persuade Chris, one of the relay team members, into going for a solo Channel swim as well, and to come along to Gozo also. Throughout the winter we had become friends and had trained together at a local pool. Chris had his own mental concerns about the Channel and I told him about hypnotherapy. We both had a session with Clem prior to the swim camp.

The night before we were due to travel to Gozo, I agreed to pick Chris up at 2 a.m. to leave for the airport. I arrived at his house and phoned him, trying not to wake the neighbours.

There was no answer. I rang again and still no answer. After approximately twenty-five missed calls I was starting to panic, thinking we would miss our plane. I tried throwing stones at his window and knocking on his door – still nothing! After forty-five minutes he eventually appeared at the window, looking dazed. Another five minutes and I would have had to leave without him. I said, 'I can't believe you didn't hear the phone or the knocking!' He told me he had put Clem's hypnotherapy CD on at 9 p.m. and was so relaxed he was in a deep sleep.

It was now a big rush to make the plane. Chris drove very fast and when we arrived we had to run through the airport. We made it with a couple of minutes to spare before the check-in desk closed.

In Gozo we were handed our schedules. With swimming sessions planned every day, it did concern me that my shoulder wouldn't cope. I wasn't used to swimming every day without a rest day in between.

The first day was a gentle late-afternoon swim around a small area close to the beach, to get us into the swing of things.

On day two we started bright and early and hugged the coast for an hour. After just twenty minutes I was stung by some sort of jellyfish; I'm not sure what kind it was but it left me with lacerations on my wrist for three weeks, which created a nice bracelet-shaped tattoo. We then had lunch on the big safety boat, and once the food had settled we swam two hours back to where our hotel was.

The swim should have been simple enough, but I started to feel seasick early on and my goggles filled up with water, which made me uneasy as I kept having to stop to adjust them. The waves were a little rocky and it caused me to vomit a few times. When I finished I was glad it was over; I hadn't enjoyed it at all. It knocked my confidence a little and I couldn't help thinking, 'It's only two hours and I'm having these problems – it doesn't bode well for my Channel swim.'

I went to bed that evening thinking about the six-hour with a little apprehension. The two-hour had been a reminder that swims weren't always going to go according to plan.

The next morning we met at the boat for 9 a.m. with everything we needed: sunscreen, Vaseline for friction, swim hat and goggles. We had a thirty-minute ride to a place called Fungi Rock, which was about one kilometre to swim around. The choice of venue was a good one as it was safe, protected from the open sea. When we arrived, the temperature was taken at 16 degrees. I tried to tell myself I had done this before and I knew how to do it. But among these thoughts I also kept thinking, 'I can't remember what 16 degrees feels like . . . I wonder if I will feel the cold.'

The group set off together and as soon as I hit the water I started analysing the temperature in detail, thinking about every part of my body as I swam and confirming to myself that I did indeed feel cold and it wasn't as warm as Dover. This was my only focus as I swam around the rock for the first hour. I couldn't get the temperature out of my mind – it was punishing me – and the more I thought about it the worse I became. I started praying to reach the warm patches where the sun was beating down on the water. The inside of the rock was quite protected and the only warm patch was at the entrance, which felt at least 1 degree warmer, but the problem was that I'd swim through it and immediately feel colder as a result. The only other way to enjoy the brief relief of warmth was by urinating as I swam, which again didn't last long, but at approximately 37 degrees Celsius was definitely worthwhile. As you can't get out to go to the toilet, why not make the most of it.

I reached the two-hour point and waited for the RIB, which was going to each swimmer in turn to give them a warm carbohydrate drink. I said to John (who was the senior guide), 'I'm freezing to death!' I sensed the look on my face was one of panic and shock. I kept thinking, 'How could I possibly feel this cold so early on in the swim.' I'm not sure what response I was expecting from John – my plan wasn't to get out and he certainly wouldn't have let me out – but I just wanted him to know how bad I felt. I was annoyed at myself for accepting that I was cold like it was a weakness and it felt like the temperature was winning. John predictably told me, 'Just keep going', and I pushed on.

The feeling of cold seeped deeper into my body and my mind, and rather than dismissing it like Clem had taught me I kept telling myself, over and over, 'It's so cold . . . I'm freezing to death . . .' My teeth started chattering, to further acknowledge how cold I was, and this then continued for the remaining four hours. The cold had well and truly taken over and I started shouting under the water, 'If you're going to kill me then come on!' It didn't seem to help. I just couldn't snap out of this mindset.

The stupid thing about it was that I knew how it felt to suffer from hypothermia and this wasn't anywhere near the same feeling I'd had then. Sure it was very uncomfortable, and it made me completely miserable, but if I had thought about it, I would have realised my body could handle it.

I made it to my three-hour drink swimming alone for the majority of the time. I had lost Chris, who I was planning to swim with, and so I had no one to distract me from the negative thoughts. I was now thinking, 'I'm only halfway . . . I'm going to die out here!' I was so miserable; it felt like pure torture. As I swam around, my only incentive was to get to the warm patch at the top of the rock – only to feel the temperature drop again. There was nothing positive about Fungi Rock. I didn't like the name and I certainly wasn't enjoying swimming around it – like a goldfish swimming in a bowl.

Somehow I passed the four-hour and then five-hour mark, still as miserable as ever. I counted the final minutes down: fifty-five, fifty, forty-five . . . I couldn't wait for it to be over. I eventually caught up with Chris, and swimming together was at least something to focus on. For the final five minutes I was constantly looking at my watch.

At last we were called in, right on the six-hour mark. It was over, thank goodness! I climbed onto the boat, threw my three thick tops on and felt like a train had run me over.

I should have been pleased that I had ticked off another six-hour swim, whereas I was actually quite stressed. This was another wake-up call. I had felt so confident from the six-hour I had completed in Dover and that confidence had just been obliterated. It was a reminder of what I was up against and brought me crashing back down to earth. I reflected on the swim, and I made a deal with myself that I would never let my teeth chatter like that again. I felt that I had succumbed to it and mentally got it all wrong.

We took the boat back to the hotel. I had been dreaming of a warm bath for most of the swim and I couldn't wait to get back and jump into the tub. I felt so cold – like it had gone right through to the bone.

I was sharing a room with Chris and we were due to meet

up with the rest of the group for a debrief. (I must admit I had not been looking forward to sharing a room with Chris – I had done so before when we trained for the Channel relay crossing and he had snored like a foghorn.) When he finished his shower he started talking to me about how tough the swim was and how tired he was. As he was chatting I suddenly realised that he was standing there completely naked, eating a chocolate bar which was like acid to my eyes! I stopped him mid-conversation and said, 'I'm happy to talk about the swim but for God's sake put some clothes on, man!' Chris started laughing, I think realising how funny it must have looked. We went to the group meeting to review the session with everyone and I couldn't resist telling them all about the chocolate-bar incident, which everyone found very funny.

The next day we'd been planning a one-and-a-half-hour warm-down swim but it had to be abandoned as some of the group were stung badly by jellyfish – including Marcus, who later became my teammate in another Channel relay. He said at one point he came out of the water with two jellyfish stuck to his goggles, as if it were a comedy sketch. As a result we changed location to a nice lagoon (with no jellyfish), did a gentle swim and had a small walk afterwards. I didn't mind – it was actually nice to have a day off as my shoulder was very painful.

I had three physio sessions in four days to get me through the camp. At least I think he was a physio . . . He was a huge mammoth of a man who crushed my back with his elbows. His session was in a diving shop, on a table with a towel thrown across it for me to lie on. The odd thing was that I was right next to the window and everyone could see me as they walked past. In fairness, he did seem to take the edge off the pain, but after each session the pain would return as soon as I started swimming again.

Although I had achieved what I'd set out to do, I couldn't help feeling a little down about my second six-hour swim; it had been much tougher than I had envisaged and I started to question myself again. It was only ten weeks until my Channel swim, after all, and I would potentially need to swim for double that length of time.

When I arrived back in the UK, I booked another session with Clem. Not only did I have the shoulder concern, I also now had the issue of water temperature to contend with. I knew I needed to think differently and not let these worries consume me.

I explained to Clem what had happened in Gozo and how it had affected my performance, we had a few sessions working on different techniques to help me. One of them was thought-stopping: having the ability to realise your mind is drifting into negative thoughts and stopping them before they build and affect your ability to continue. We also looked at the issue of cold water and how to combat it. He suggested I visualise being warm and swimming in a warm ring, the rationale being that if you pictured yourself doing this you couldn't also be thinking you were cold. I made the decision not to use the word 'cold' any more, as if it didn't exist – it wasn't a real word so I couldn't possibly feel that way.

The first time I'd come to see Clem I had told him that I was worried my shoulder would not be capable of making the swim. As I was telling him this, I would touch my shoulder in acknowledgement of the pain. He said, 'Whenever you talk about your shoulder you touch it, which reminds you of your pain.' It was as if I was giving it power over me without realising it. I was focusing on it too much and therefore it was becoming a bad habit. After that, I made a conscious effort not to talk about my shoulder and not to touch it any more.

I felt much better after the second session with Clem, and learning mental focusing techniques really seemed to help me get back on track. I was looking forward to using these methods in training. After Gozo my shoulder was very sore and although I wasn't overly focusing on it, I knew it was important to rest for an entire week to allow the pain to settle. This was tough as I knew other Channel-swimming aspirants were training all the time. I just had to accept my limitations and not allow the setback to affect my belief that I would achieve the swim.

I made the decision not to go to Dover until the third week of May, opting instead to work hard in the pool over shorter distances, doing high-tempo three-quarter-pace swim sets with limited rests. These had served me well over the last eighteen months, improving my speed and stamina. It was also good to save energy by not doing the seven-hour round trip to Dover, while the lake in early May was still only 8 degrees – a couple of thirty-minute swims there would not have been the best use of my time.

At the weekends I would instead test how long I could hold a strong pace for, monitoring my time every 100 metres over 8–10 kilometres. I would also do non-stop three-hour swims on one of the days. Weekends for me became training, eating and resting, then more training before going back to work on the Monday.

On the third weekend in May, Chris and I went to Dover. The temperature was 11.5 degrees and we swam twice, doing one and a half hours the first time, then out to get warm, and then another hour for the second swim. This somehow seemed worse than doing a straight two and a half hours, as we had to get warm and then go through the body shock again. It was good acclimatisation training, which was necessary to get our bodies used to the temperature.

There were around twenty people on the beach braving the water, some of them seasoned cold-water swimmers. You could see who the less experienced ones were as they were shivering uncontrollably, turning blue, and some had tears running down their faces. The cold has a way of affecting you like nothing else I've experienced, but the more dips you have the easier it becomes.

I thought I'd put my new mental focus to the test and fake my way into thinking the cold wasn't a problem. Chris and I walked into the water with the others and we joked about how warm it was, whereas the majority of them walked in with a visible sense of impending doom. Chris and I were fake-smiling as if we were in 35-degree heat on a beach in Spain, about to have a nice cooling dip.

We started off swimming to the left-hand pier wall, as I had done previously. When we reached the first wall, and before I could even say anything, Chris said, 'It's lovely and warm, isn't it?' It was just me around and I thought, 'You don't have to fool me, Chris.' I didn't say much, though, trying to gauge whether or not he was feeling the cold. I tried thinking about swimming in the warm ring, as Clem had taught me, although what was in my mind was that Chris was handling the temperature better than me. I started to think, 'Why am I so cold, then?' I tried to stop the thought and instead visualise being warm again. We swam to the opposite wall and he said the same again: 'I can't believe how warm it is!' By now I was a little irritated. I didn't think he was warm; we were in our swim shorts and unless he was made out of polar-bear fur he would be feeling it like I was.

In reality he was just faking it better, and not only fooling me but also trying to fool himself – so there was method in the madness. It started to make me think that other swimmers could handle the temperature better than I could. It's strange how the thought of Chris coping with the temperature made it worse, somehow. Maybe that was just my competitive side coming out.

I began chanting, with every stroke, 'Warm, hot, warm', 'Hot, hot, warm' and other similar alternatives – you would be amazed at how many variations of those two words you can put together. It may seem a very simple and uninteresting strategy, saying that to yourself over and over again, but it seemed after a while to be working. As Clem taught me: you can't think negative while you're thinking positive. It's impossible. I realised that if I continued to say in my head I was warm then I was shutting out any chance of negative cold thoughts entering my mind. It might seem obvious, but it turned out to be a revelation, and if it worked for temperature it could surely work on other things such as my shoulder and the will to succeed. I tested the theory by stopping saying and thinking about any words associated with being warm for a minute and having blank thoughts, and sure enough my mind started drifting into how cold it was, which confirmed the need to do it.

I had learned a lot from this swim: the importance of fooling myself and the power of positive words. Not treating the swim too seriously seemed the best strategy. I now believed that if something was achievable in your mind it was achievable in reality.

As open-water swimming is such a mental game, arguably 80 per cent mental and 20 per cent physical, if your head isn't in the right place then it will try to get the better of you. I have seen open-water swimmers who can swim all day by themselves when there's no pressure, but on the day of their Channel swim, when it matters, the moment gets hold of them and they cannot replicate what they've achieved in training due to self-doubt and negative thoughts. Open-water swimming is cruel like that; it is one of the most uncompromising sports there is. If you have any gaps in your armour, including emotional baggage, an ocean swim has a way of reminding you of it and eking out the weaknesses. When you are alone with your thoughts and limited stimulus, and you're feeling physically tired, that's when the devil on your shoulder wakes up to remind you that it hurts, it's cold, it's too far and you should quit.

I was looking forward to the next weekend in Dover as I knew the distance would be increased and it would be another good test. I arrived and the conversation on the beach revolved around the same topic as the previous week: how cold it was. If you ask most open-water swimmers what their primary concern is, they will inevitably say temperature, due to the discomfort and pain it can cause. This week it had increased to 12.5–13 degrees and Freda gave Chris and me a three-hour swim. Although the temperature had increased by around a degree from the previous week, it was still going to be cold; three hours in that temperature would feel a very long time. But on this occasion I was determined to keep saying positive words to myself, over and over again.

As I waded in, I again tried to look at the positive side: it was slightly warmer, so it would be easier. As we swam off, it took me a few minutes to immerse my face, which is one of the more sensitive parts of the body to the cold. When I became more experienced, I learned that by wetting the back of my neck and face, and then putting my shoulders under in a systematic fashion without too much delay, I was priming my body for entry and it wasn't too much of a shock to the system.

I took my time to the first wall, getting my arms moving gradually and feeling my way through the water. Chris was alongside me and when we arrived at the wall, just like last time, he said, 'I can't believe how warm it is.' I thought, 'Not again – I'm not falling for it this time!' I just said, 'Yeah, it is.' I started early, tuning into positive thinking again, visualising being warm, telling myself, 'I am a winner, a champion' – anything to divert from the reality of what was happening. The power of positive thinking worked, and although it wasn't pleasant, three hours were successfully completed.

We stayed overnight in Folkestone and did another three hours the following day. This time I planned to get my own back on Chris, and as we reached the first harbour wall I beat him to it.

'I can't believe how warm it is!' I exclaimed.

He said, 'You're joking, right?'

'No,' I said. 'The last few swims you were telling me how warm it was and only now have I realised you're right. It's like a swimming pool. It's unbelievable. I'm loving it. Come on, let's keep going!' I was playing him at his own game.

After a couple of hours of me doing this, Chris said, looking quite miserable, 'I don't think it's that warm, to be honest.'

I said to him, 'Look how still my hands are – I'm not even shaking!' What he didn't realise was that my legs were shaking vigorously underneath. It was amazing, the effect it had on him: like me, he felt worse thinking someone was coping better than he was.

As I had by now completed two six-hour swims, three hours seemed much more manageable. I think it's easier to convince yourself to carry on when you have swum a longer distance, as there is no excuse to quit.

I had successfully completed another open-water swim and I sensed the following week we'd be up to six hours in a water temperature of around 13 degrees. I had never swum for that long in that temperature before, so I knew it would call on all my mental strength.

11

THE TRIALS AND TRIBULATIONS OF A CHANNEL SWIMMER

I thought about my next challenge all week at work and was excited. It was now June and my Channel swim was only six weeks away. I knew I had to complete every swim Freda set, as I had with all my previous swims. Developing good winning habits was the key for me, leaving no doubt at all of my capability to get across. Success breeds more success, I thought, and I had to keep ticking these swims off.

Chris and I were late in leaving home the following week and it was a rush to get to Dover on time. We had to run and get changed quickly to catch up with the others. Freda looked like she was going to kill us, so we didn't hang around. I needed to go to the bathroom but there was no time for that.

We started our swim and within thirty minutes I really needed to go for a 'number two'. I kept thinking, 'How am I going to hold on for six hours?' I tried to block it out of my mind. I reached an hour and thirty minutes and I couldn't hang on any longer – I was so desperate to go. The problem is that when you are face down in the water, you are forced to relax your pelvic floor, and so if you need to go . . . you need to go! Chris was swimming next to me and I slowed down to allow him to carry on without me. Normally he would just keep on going, but this time he saw me treading water. It was so embarrassing but I had no choice. Chris made his way back to me and said, 'What are you doing?'

'Nothing,' I said. 'Keep swimming, mate, and I'll catch you up!'

He replied, 'You're not doing what I think you're doing, are you?' When I denied it he responded, 'You are!'

I was mortified and asked him to not mention it to anyone. He agreed and we continued swimming. Within a couple of minutes we passed another swimmer whom we both knew called Ben, and he said, 'Hi lads – temperature's not too bad, is it?'

Chris replied, 'He's just gone for a dump in here!'

The look on Ben's face was a picture. He replied with, 'Oh, great', put his goggles down and continued swimming. I wanted to kill Chris for doing that to me. I continued swimming with my trunks around my ankles for the next 1.4 kilometres, shivering and giggling at the same time. I thought this was the best method due to the circumstances. The only positive of this situation was that it distracted me from the temperature. I went on to complete the six-hour and Chris took great joy in telling everyone on the beach what had happened which was extremely embarrassing.

This wasn't the worst experience I had in training - that came the following week. The same thing happened again with my stomach, while doing another 6 hour swim and after three hours I stopped to tread water. I also had a nosebleed and a headache, I was bent over double with stomach ache, I was vomiting and now I was also shivering from being motionless. I was desperate to get out – I couldn't take any more. I thought, 'How can I convince Freda that it's OK for me to come out?' I had hit rock-bottom mentally and had to find a way to carry on. I remember hearing a story about a giant of a man who was training to swim the English Channel and wanted to get out because he was so cold. He came out of the water in tears in one session, begging to get changed, and Freda marched him by his trunks back into the water. I thought at the time how mean it was, now I realise tough methods like that are required when you are facing such extreme conditions.

I knew I couldn't give myself an option to get out so I made a deal with myself: do one more hour and assess again. I was really shaking as I swam; the cold had got to me. When I reached the four-hour mark I said to myself, 'One more hour, then you're on the final stretch.' It was tough – I was in a world of hurt and mentally breaking down, and every now and then I started my old trick of yelling in the water like a crazy person: 'If you want to kill me then come on!' I realised I had developed this love/hate relationship with the ocean and shouting every now and then made me somehow feel better.

I wanted to develop the mindset of never having an option to get out of the water. If I showed any sort of weakness, I could do it again and again. I needed to get into a positive habit of completing every training swim.

I managed again to incentivise myself to keep going and make it to the last hour. In my open-water training sessions the final stretch had always seemed easier than the previous hours, but there was nothing easy about this swim. The psychology of knowing that you are near the end gives you the incentive to push and complete the swim. I was desperate to finish and when I finally did it was a massive relief. I quickly got dressed and sat in my car, shivering uncontrollably, and when I glanced at my watch and thought, 'I have to do this all again tomorrow, in fourteen hours' time', it was the last thing on earth I wanted to do.

I went back to the hotel and couldn't wait to collapse in a hot bath. My shoulder was so sore and I could see in the mirror that it was slightly raised on the bad side, which was most probably as a result of unconsciously hunching to protect it when I was swimming. The pain was like a dull ache running down my arm into my biceps, which became a regular feature during my training. The longer I went, the worse it became.

The next day I woke up very sore and uncomfortable and I had to do a five-hour swim. I was dreading it. I started the swim very slowly and tried to work around my injury. This became a common issue throughout: where to position my hands to avoid irritating the shoulder. It was an added challenge I didn't need. There was nothing I could do about it and I managed to complete the five hours, albeit struggling to lift my arm for much of the time; it was just collapsing out in front and of no real use in propelling me forward.

All week I rested it in preparation for the following weekend. I was so worried throughout training that the damage I was doing might prevent me from completing my Channel swim. I kept praying for my shoulder to be good enough to get me across – I was willing to accept the damage as a result.

The next few weeks were characterised by pretty much no swimming during the week but longer swims at the weekend. On one of the swims I did seven hours, from which I emerged looking a blue-grey colour and even Freda asked me if I was OK. I did six or seven long swims in total before my due date of 10 July. During the last couple of weeks I limited my training as I wanted my shoulder to be in the best shape possible. The first week in July I was so sore I just floated in Dover Harbour for two hours doing a little backstroke and nothing else.

The swim was so close now and the nerves were growing. Concern for my shoulder was in the forefront of my mind and I desperately tried to keep it under control. Even though I felt mentally strong, I couldn't help having the occasional thought of, 'What if the shoulder goes?' Those thoughts were few and far between as I had trained myself to block them out and focus on the positives. I knew this was my protective mechanism and I switched my mind to thinking about swimming in simple terms: just one arm in front of the other. You can always do another arm stroke, no matter how tired or sore you are – it's just one more arm.

On 7 July I travelled back to Dover in readiness for the swim. The weather was not looking good for the 10th. I had heard things can change very quickly with the Channel, and so you have to be prepared. Unfortunately, it quickly became apparent that the weather would not improve for me. After two nights in Dover I thought I might as well go home and wait for the following week. I travelled home on my thirtieth birthday. The rain was belting down and it was such a miserable day all round. I was really down.

This sport keeps you on a knife's edge; you convince yourself you're going to swim, get yourself prepared mentally and physically, and then you're told, 'No, sorry, the weather conditions aren't good enough and we will have to wait for another date, and even then you won't know if it'll actually happen.' Some people train really hard during the week, sacrifice so much, and yet they might not get a chance at an attempt that year. It is cruel, and it tests your mental focus and composure as you need to be ready to go at the drop of a hat. I have seen accomplished swimmers who are both physically and mentally prepared, but their swims are cancelled again and again and the anxiety starts to creep in. By the time they eventually go, they have lost that focus and they set off with self-doubt, which quickly overpowers them and they convince themselves to give up. It is not like competing in a pool swimming gala, where the date and time is set and unless the leisure centre burns down the race will go ahead. Here you are in Mother Nature's hands, and if she decides you're not going, you're not going!

The worst thing for me was going back to work and trying to focus on my job. All I could think about was when I would be swimming the Channel. It felt like I was waiting on death row for my fate. I went back to work for three days and the swim never left my mind for more than a few seconds. I was even invited to a Michelin-starred restaurant with a customer, which at any other time I would really have looked forward to, but the last thing I wanted to do was travel a few hours to watch everyone else drink while I sipped on water. (I had not drunk alcohol for the last six months.) The restaurant had a taster menu called 'Sounds of the Sea', which was served with an iPod in a shell; as you ate your meal you listened to the sounds of the ocean waves splashing against the shore. This was the last thing in the world I wanted to hear only a few days before my Channel swim! It did make me smile, though, watching one couple having a romantic meal, both with headphones in their ears, listening to the ocean.

Two days later I was told there was a chance of going on 14 July. It was now the 12th and I was to ring in the morning. When I rang Mike, the pilot, he said there was a fifty-fifty chance, based on the weather, and what did I want to do? I asked for more detail to try to make a decision, but ultimately it was up to me and I was no clearer on whether to go or not. Mike said Lance, his son, was out with another swimmer in the Channel and suggested I phone again in the evening and he would tell me what it had been like. I had all my bags ready in the lounge and didn't know what to do – there were so many things to arrange. By the evening it would be too late to find someone to look after the dogs and cats and even then there might still be no guarantee of when I'd actually go.

I was stressed and I sat on my sofa and clock-watched for the next eight hours until it hit 6 p.m. and I could phone Lance – who didn't pick up. I tried again thirty minutes later and got through to him. He asked me what I wanted to do.

I said, 'Your dad said I should ask you.'

'Well, it's fifty-fifty,' he replied. 'What do you want to do?'

I just made the decision in that moment: 'I'll come.'

Lance told me that he would pass on the message and we would try for the next morning. I made some quick arrangements to book the hotel and called my brother to come on my boat. I also managed to get the pets sorted and finally left home after 8.30 p.m. I arrived in Folkestone just before midnight. I was due to meet Mike at 7 a.m. and I hoped I would get some sleep.

12

SWIM #1 ENGLISH CHANNEL – THE FIRST TEST

I did sleep for a few hours, which surprised me considering the pressure I was under. At 5 a.m. I had the sudden realisation that I was going to swim all day and take on the toughest challenge I had ever embarked on. I tried to remain calm and after a couple of nervous trips to the bathroom I made my way to the harbour.

Driving from Folkestone to Dover was a short ten-minute trip, but I felt so many emotions as I approached and the sea suddenly appeared. So many times I had driven to Dover in training and gone over the brow of the hill where the sea becomes visible and felt my heart sink to the ground, knowing I would be immersed for six hours before being able to come back out. This time the feeling was much worse and my objective was to keep as calm as possible. I would tell myself, 'This is the final training session, Adam – this is what you have been working towards and after this you never have to do it again.' On all those training sessions I had given myself so many incentives to keep going – never having to do it again was the biggest one of all!

In amongst all the nerves there was an element of excitement and a feeling of pride. I was about to swim the longest distance I had ever swum, across the English Channel, the busiest shipping lane in the world. Inside I felt like someone special for once, unique. I thought about all the hard work I had done to get there and I felt very determined. The nerves were there all right, but there was no self-doubt. For the last eighteen months, everything had been building up to this moment, and I would finally test my capability. I was up for it more than I had ever been up for anything in my life, feeling well prepared and trying to convince myself I could do it. I knew I could swim six hours – now I just needed to do that twice!

My team all met on the boat: my brother Mark, my wife, my friend and training partner Chris, and Jim whom I'd met at the swim training camp in Gozo and who had become a good friend. Mike complained that we had a lot of equipment, but my thinking had been that it was better to be prepared for every eventuality. We had lots of snacks, including Jelly Babies, chocolate rolls and my two kilograms of carbohydrate powder; I planned to feed on the first hour and then every half hour afterwards, so I worked out I could be drinking up to twenty-five litres of fluid. We also had a safety kit, which included plasters, antihistamine cream for jellyfish stings, blankets if I became hypothermic, light sticks if it got dark, and lots of jumpers, tops, jackets and a woolly hat for when I got out.

As in the relay, there are two possible starting points for a solo Channel crossing: Samphire Hoe and Shakespeare Beach. My starting point was Shakespeare Beach, the same as for the relay, and it would take around twenty minutes to get there by boat. Jim had the worst job in open-water swimming: putting on the plastic gloves and rubbing Vaseline behind my neck and under my arms. This is done to stop rubbing and chafing from all the arm rotations, as I would be averaging around seventy thousand swim strokes across the duration. (I didn't do it myself as it was important not to get Vaseline on my hands in case I touched my goggles and couldn't see – well, that was my excuse, anyway).

When we came within 75 metres of the shore, I took a deep breath in and then out. I tried not to think of anything in order to keep my mind clear from any negative thoughts and stay calm. This was not the time for self-doubt or any mental glitches. I was aware I wouldn't be coming out of the water all day, but I couldn't allow that to dominate my mind.

I jumped in, and as my legs broke the water I sensed how cool it felt, but as quickly as I sensed it the feeling went away as my brain was engaged on the job in hand. All the training in similar and colder temperatures had prepped me for this. I felt that my thoughts were in check and I was in a strong, secure mindset, not allowing my protective mechanism to creep in and make me aware of the reality I was about to face.

I remember thinking in the relay that it was a little harsh having to swim to shore and clear the water before you can even start. I had thought I would just be magically airlifted and placed directly onto the beach – wishful thinking!

I felt pretty calm, though, considering I had put so much effort into getting here. I knew what I had to do. I didn't want to put an anticipated time on the crossing, as the Channel isn't a still body of water and you cannot predict what will happen. I prepared myself mentally to do whatever it took.

I turned to face the boat and raised my arms in the air to show I had cleared the water. I can see how those few minutes alone, staring out to sea and waiting to start, could affect people on long-distance swims – the mind trying to wander with the realisation of what you are about to do.

This was it, then. What had I let myself in for? It had all started with a fictional movie and a crazy idea that was now real life – there was no turning back. I waited for the signal – a siren from the boat – and then Mike shouted, 'Hit the water!'

I dived in as if I were in a mad rush or a race against time, which wasn't a great approach considering I would no doubt be out there all day. The adrenaline was flowing and I wanted to start with the right intent. I remember thinking, 'Am I going too fast? Can I keep this pace up?' As I had never swum this distance before, I started analysing my speed, all the time trying to shut out any demons at the back of my mind who were trying to question my approach.

I found it comfortable breathing to the right-hand side, so I swam to the left of the boat. As I made my way out into the ocean, I started feeling the choppy water. Most of my training had been in flat, calm water, so it felt a little strange being knocked about.

Forty-five minutes into the swim, the waves continued to knock me around, although I started to relax and still retained a fast pace. The initial adrenaline had died down and I got into my zone, switching off mentally. I even stuck my tongue out at the boat to relax myself and show everyone I was enjoying it, or at least trying to fool myself. In a strange way I *was* enjoying it – for the first time in my life I felt really proud of what I was embarking on, which made me happy to be out there. I was determined to not let the moment overcome me; I had to embrace it. I knew these moments in life don't happen very often.

We had brought a whiteboard as I wanted to be notified when there were five minutes to go before a feed, as we'd done with changeovers in the Channel relay. 'The feed' is a Channel-swimming term meaning a drink or solid food, depending on how I was feeling. At fifty-five minutes the board went up and I made sure I was close to the boat so as to not waste any time when the drinks bottle was thrown to me. Prior to the swim I had been told about the importance of a quick feed, the reason being that those seconds can make all the difference with the tide towards the end of the swim – if you're too slow you might have to swim several more hours before the tide changes again and eventually lets you in to land.

The whiteboard went up with FEED written on it with black marker pen. The first one was two scoops of a carbohydrate powder topped up with 500 millilitres of water and blackcurrant. The drink was lowered down to me in a sports bottle attached to a piece of rope, as the rules decreed I could not touch the boat. I was conscious of time so I quickly grabbed the bottle, put my head back and squeezed in as much liquid as I could, pretty much finishing the whole bottle in around twenty seconds. I knew the taste and it was definitely not a drink I looked forward to, but I knew it would give me a slow release of energy and it was important for me to take on fuel. I treated it like a military operation: no time to speak, just consume as much as possible, drop the bottle and continue. So far so good, I thought. My crew pulled the bottle back up to the boat and would rinse it out ready for drink number two.

The next hour was very much like the first and went by with very little trouble, apart from the choppy water making me feel seasick. One hour and fifty-five minutes into the swim, it was the same procedure as before: the whiteboard came up with a 5 written on it and five minutes later, on the two-hour mark, I stopped as the drinks bottle was thrown to me.

Shortly after the second feed, the water started to become rougher. It was as if I was swimming in a washing machine and I felt increasingly sick. At two hours fifteen minutes I couldn't hold back any more and started vomiting. I had been sick a number of times in training and knew there was a chance it could happen at some point during my crossing – I just hadn't thought it would be so early in the swim. I was now on feeds every half-hour, from two hours thirty minutes onwards. I hoped that by the next feed my stomach would have settled. But this wasn't the case. I couldn't hold anything down so when it came, it was of no benefit at all; the drink came out of me as quickly as it went in. This continued to happen for up to four hours. I tried a scoop of electrolyte powder with hot chocolate to help with hydration, which also didn't work and came out of me almost instantly.

I was now really worried and had to ask myself, 'If I can't hold anything down, how can I possibly finish this swim?' I thought about how I was burning approximately 1,100 calories an hour. Even a full bottle of carbohydrate drink is only around 600 calories. Therefore I would be losing around 500 calories an hour with the drink. If I am sick and not replacing those calories my body will be looking for fuel to burn, like muscle and fat.

At four and a half hours, just after being sick again, I thought the swim was all over in my mind. It was the first time I had allowed any doubts into my head about not making the crossing. My mind just became possessed with negative thoughts, convincing me that it was physically impossible to carry on without food. I went into a panic state and felt really upset. It was a disaster. I had done so much training and had swum longer than this before, yet I was now telling myself it could be over and there was no point in continuing. This was the first test and it was a big one.

I started talking to myself: 'How much do you want it, Adam? Do you really want it enough?' The answer was clear. I imagined my dad on the boat and visualised his face saying to me, 'Don't you give up – give it everything you've got!' This is what had driven me on during those gruelling training sessions – not giving up – and it served me well now too. I also thought about the people who had sponsored me and the time away from home, as well as the money spent on getting me here. I had personally saved up for this, putting money to one side, and my parents had also helped fund the crossing. I didn't want them to waste their money or to feel I had let them down, even though they wouldn't have thought that way. I had to clear my head and focus on one thing. I made the decision at that moment that I just didn't have a choice. I said, 'Adam, if the boat wasn't there you would have to swim across. If you had to swim it to save your family, you would. Now get going!'

From that moment on, I made a deal with myself that I would continue with the swim whatever it threw at me. Failure was not an option. This meant too much to me. I carried on swimming.

Before the next feed, my crew asked Mike some advice on what to give me to settle the sickness. He said, 'Just give him plain water and one scoop of carbohydrate powder and tell him it's just water.' This turned out to be a great decision. I came in for the feed and they told me just that. It did taste a little strange for water, but when your mouth has been in salt water for a while nothing tastes quite as it should. Either way, it did the trick: I believed them and didn't have the negative mental association with vomiting. I wasn't sure whether the sickness was down to motion or physically pushing myself – or maybe a bit of both.

My stomach finally settled down for the first time in two and a half hours. I remembered that a friend of mine, Sean Burns, had sponsored me £1 for every time I was sick. I thought, 'Well, he owes me twenty pounds, so it's not all bad. Happy days!'

I was now feeling much better physically and it had a knock-on mental effect too. It was strange, the changing emotions going from thinking the swim was over to feeling physically fine again. The experience taught me a lot about how things can improve and change if you stick with it and battle through.

There was no danger of the conditions letting up, though; they were here to stay and the ocean gods were determined to test my capabilities and remind me why this swim was so tough. The day before my Channel crossing, a friend who was in the military had told me that a navy friend of his said the wind would pick up after a few hours and could reach up to 20 knots by the afternoon. I had been advised that if the wind in knots is double figures at the start of the swim, they normally won't take a swimmer across. But the wind, like the ocean, can be unpredictable; it was me who made the final decision to go, so I had no complaints.

I pushed on with the swim and now the sickness had

stopped, I started giving myself positive affirmations as Clem had taught me to, telling myself things like, 'You're strong, you're powerful, you are a winner', over and over again. I was determined that the mental demons wouldn't return and while I was saying positive words I couldn't be thinking negatively.

As I reached six hours, Jim jumped into the water to swim with me and give me some support. According to the rules, you are allowed another swimmer in the water with you after three hours, and every two hours after that if you require it. He or she must not touch you, must ideally stay just behind you and can swim for up to one hour. In Jim's case, however, he started swimming strongly, as if it were an hour's sprint, and flew past me in no time, which did nothing for my positive mindset. Jim is a slower swimmer than me and I think he thought he would have to go flat-out to keep up, but after six hours I had lost some of my pace. He started swimming away from the boat towards Belgium at one point, which was quite funny. It was nice to have some company and I would rather have had him in the water than not as it did help me to pick up my speed.

Jim was great support throughout, sitting low down towards the middle of the boat and encouraging me to swim close so that the boat could protect me from the choppy water. He would shout, 'Swim in the box, Adam.' He would also clap to keep my spirits up. It does make such a difference to have that encouragement when you are alone with just your thoughts for company and only a boat to look at; any kind of stimulus can really help keep your spirits high.

My brain wanted to keep occupied, but at the same time I didn't want to think too much about what was going on in case it turned into a negative. As I swam I did start to wonder what they were talking about on the boat, and any noise or smells became the height of entertainment for me, as they were a break from thinking about one arm then the other. At one stage the pilot and co-pilot started cooking bacon. I was swimming at the front of the boat and the waft that came out was quite nice. The co-pilot had his leg out on deck as if he were on a relaxing, scenic boat cruise. At one stage I shouted out, 'Can I have one of those, please?' To which the response was an immediate 'No!'

At the eight-hour mark I came in for a feed. I started drinking flat Coke as I had heard it was good for settling the stomach and it was my only alternative to the carbohydrate powder. I was beyond drink, though, at this stage – it was almost not worth having it as I consumed so little and spat it out straight away.

I asked the crew, 'How long to go?' and the co-pilot responded, 'About three miles.'

I then saw my crew give him a stern look, as if to say, 'I'm not sure you should be telling him that.' The reason being that most people give up at the 3-mile marker as it is the point where the tide and currents can be the most unpredictable. It is not like doing 3 miles in the pool or a still lake, where the flow of water will not change. Even though I knew this, my brain quickly computed that I would easily finish in another hour and thirty minutes, no problem, as my speed was quick enough; with the tides normally changing every six hours, I didn't believe they would affect me and so I'd be likely to finish in nine hours thirty minutes.

The one and a half hours became my target – just three more feeds and I would be reaching for land in France. The conditions were still bad, with a lot of choppy waves, but I felt I had done the worst of it and it would be straightforward from now on.

At nine hours I took a glimpse ahead. It still seemed a good distance to reach land. I had been taking glances at France from the four-hour mark, even though Freda had told me in Dover, 'Whatever you do, don't look at France during the swim as it always looks closer than it is and once you look you won't stop!' She was right. I couldn't help it. I still convinced myself that in thirty minutes' time I would be in France, as that is what I had been told.

At nine hours thirty minutes, the time I'd calculated I'd be finishing, I came in for another feed. It annoyed me that it was as if nothing had previously been said about me being so close to the land. By this time I was panting quite hard.

I said, 'How long to go?'

The response from the co-pilot: 'Three miles.'

'Another three miles!' I said. 'Oh no!'

The response back from Chris: 'Shut up, it's only three miles!'

I didn't have any energy to argue, although I was annoyed at being told to shut up, but he was only trying to help. This was the first time I had said anything negative; until now I had been quiet to save my energy as I didn't want to show any weakness and allow negativity to creep in. I was just frustrated, as I couldn't believe the information had been so wrong.

Jim then said, 'Adam, it's just this last final step – you know how to do it!'

Chris then added, 'We are all really proud of you.'

Both comments gave me a huge lift and this was just what I needed. It is amazing how powerful, positive words can have such an impact on you. Whenever I support swimmers on a

Channel crossing now I make sure they clearly see and hear positive body and verbal language. If they believe the swim is going wrong in any way, they might give up.

I swam off to the sound of some claps from my crew, which gave me goosebumps. I had learned my lesson and switched off any thoughts of how much longer it could take. I went back to just swimming and keeping my mind clear. 'Just swim feed to feed, Adam,' I would tell myself. Once I got over the disappointment of not completing the swim within ten hours, I started thinking about the positives. Every minute I swam now was more than I had ever done before. My previous longest duration in open water had been seven hours. This strategy worked really well to relax me and got me back into my zone.

Another thirty minutes and I came in again for a feed. I didn't say anything this time as I was breathing quite heavily and I consumed very little. That didn't matter, though – it was beneficial just to come in and hear positive words from my crew. As soon as that feed was done, it seemed the next one came along. The last few hours were ticking away quickly, now that my mind was clear and not focusing on how long I had still to go. Clem had spoken to me about time distortion and how to think of each hour as only a few minutes. It is very much similar to everyday life: when you are really enjoying yourself and fully engaged, you lose track of time. I wouldn't say that in this case I was really enjoying it, but I switched off and thought only about putting one arm in front of the other.

I came in on the eleven-hour mark – I knew it was around this time as I had counted each feed and it was twenty in total. (If I had consumed 500 millilitres every time that would have been ten litres of fluid. The European Food Safety Authority recommends that you drink two litres on a normal day. Then again, this was far from a normal day.) But as I came in this time, Chris and Jim said the words I had been waiting for since the start: 'This will be your last feed.' For so long I had badly wanted to hear those words, but still I told myself to ignore them and just keep swimming. After the disappointment at 3 miles to go, I didn't want to hear any last-minute issues.

I looked up at my brother Mark and he still had the concerned look on his face that he had had for the whole swim; maybe I wasn't as close as the others were making out. I knew Mark wouldn't be able to relax until I had completed it, as he desperately wanted me to succeed. Another fifteen minutes and French soil looked very close. I remembered the last part of the movie *On a Clear Day*, where Frank is swimming in to the finish; I now had a very similar view. The water somehow felt thinner to pull back and the waves had completely flattened off. I sensed I was within a kilometre of finishing. 'Focus. Adam, focus!' I would tell myself.

Another fifteen minutes went by and France now looked desperately close. I was in a metronome state: one arm in front of the other. Mike called out to me: 'Adam, in front of you is a beach. Clear the water and then swim back.'

I couldn't believe it. I looked forward and there it was, clear as day. I was a little confused as I was expecting to land at Cap Gris Nez, which is the nearest point to Dover and full of rocks; I never envisaged swimming onto a beach. I started to get a shiver down my spine and knew the pressure was off – there was no way I wasn't going to make it now. I could enjoy the last few minutes. A huge weight had been lifted off my shoulders and I didn't feel as tired as I thought I had been.

I could finally see the seabed for the first time in eleven and a half hours, and I knew I could stand up. I wanted to swim every last drop of water, though, and then suddenly I found myself on my front with no water left. I pushed myself up onto my feet and again the movie that had inspired this swim was running through my head. I had watched it maybe a hundred times and I knew every part of it. In the movie Frank gets to his feet and falls backwards, and that must have been imprinted on my mind. I stood up and expected to be dizzier than I was. Then for no real reason I fell backwards, which was completely unnecessary, really, but the movie was so vivid in my mind and looking back it seemed a fitting end to the swim.

I walked onto the beach and only realised then that Chris and Jim had jumped in to swim the final 150 metres, which was allowed by the rules as long as they didn't touch me until I cleared the water. It was nice to have them swim in with me.

Once I cleared the water Chris turned to me and said, 'You've done it, mate!'

I didn't know what to do. I could hardly believe it. Before the swim I thought I might shout and do a big celebration, maybe run across the beach. My head couldn't really compute what had happened. In the end I just stood there and tried to soak it all in, which was impossible. It was a very surreal feeling.

In some way, in among the happiness of achieving my goal, there was also a little sadness. It seemed crazy – why on earth would I feel like that! For so long I had dreamt about this moment and for eleven hours and thirty-five minutes all I had wanted to do was finish and complete the swim. Perhaps it was the realisation that my epic battle to achieve this dream was over and I had to go back to normal life. Or perhaps I

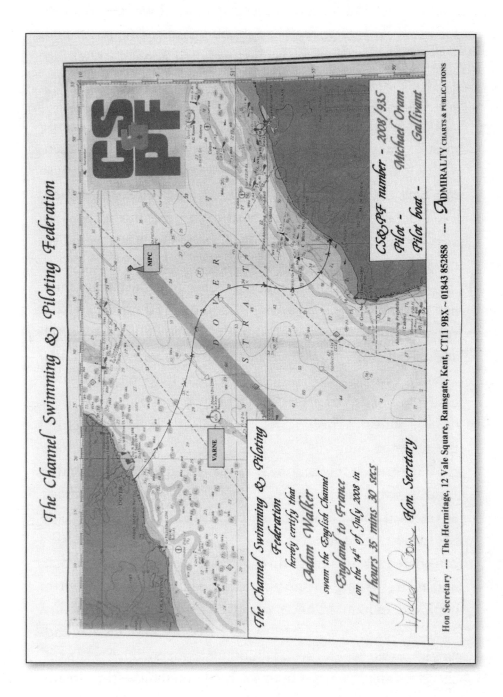

was worried that it was the end of long-distance swimming for me – something that had dominated my life and filled a void that I struggled for so many years to fill.

As I stood there on the beach, a French family walked by and the man said, 'Have you just swum from England?'

'I don't know,' I answered. 'I think so!' I started to question myself – maybe I had just dreamt that I swam the Channel.

The man asked if he and his family could get a picture with me; I felt really honoured to be asked. Chris took the picture, which I have to confess did not portray me in a good light, swollen blotchy face with an egg-shaped tan line from where my pink swim hat had covered the rest of my skin. It's fair to say it was not my finest photographic moment. The family left and I thought, 'What happens now?' The rules are that you are allowed ten minutes on the beach before the French authorities can ask you to leave. Before the swim I had found it really funny that I had to take my passport on the boat in case I was asked to prove my identity. It was a good job they didn't come and check it now as I looked very different from the passport photo.

Mike shouted for me to swim back to the boat. I really didn't want to swim one more stroke, but I didn't have much choice as the boat couldn't get in any closer and it's not as if I could board a plane on the beach and fly back to the UK. I hadn't considered needing to do this, and even though it was less than 100 metres away, all the adrenaline had been sucked out of me; even swimming one more metre seemed a major task. I swam a very slow head-up breaststroke. My arms felt as if they had lead weights on them. I could see my crew celebrating and cheering, and I climbed onto the boat and dried off.

I was really hungry and not as tired as I thought I would

be. I ate a couple of chocolate rolls and was immediately sick. My stomach was still not ready for food. On the way back to Dover, Mark was inside on the lower deck, which would have been warmer but being down there made me feel worse. I stayed outside at the back of the boat in the fresh air. I didn't feel too cold, considering; it was just that my shoulders hurt and in particular down my left bicep tendon, which was really sore. During the swim I hardly noticed the pain; I was so focused on getting across. Now the pressure was off, my brain could relax and I was reminded of the injury.

The boat took around two and a half hours to get back and I was so excited to talk to my parents and tell them the news. I hadn't realised that Mark had phoned throughout the swim to keep them updated and had stayed on the phone for the last few hundred metres so that they could get a running commentary. Mark has always been very thoughtful like that and was conscious that they would have been worried about my safety.

As I stepped off the boat back in the UK, it seemed very strange that I had just swum to another country. We went straight back to the hotel in Folkestone; I was really looking forward to a shower. The three things I always wished for the most after training for long periods of time in open water were: 1. a shower; 2. food; and 3. sleep. Normally in that order of priority. There is nothing quite like getting in a shower after feeling mildly hypothermic.

We ordered large pizzas all round and I felt so ready for proper food. But when it arrived I couldn't actually eat any. My brain wanted it, but my body wasn't so sure; my stomach felt so uncomfortable from all the sickness. I really did enjoy the shower, though – it was amazing!

The next morning I was due back at work, which was over five hours away. I phoned my boss and asked if I could come back in a couple of days. I had already taken most of my twenty-five days' holiday allocation so I was pushing it, but my boss, Tim, was very supportive and allowed me to have an extra day's rest.

I checked and found I had raised £1,200 for the Make-A-Wish Foundation and £500 for a Cats Protection home. Things couldn't be better.

13

I NEED ANOTHER CHALLENGE

When I drove back to work I was the happiest I've ever been. I felt fantastic. One of the office girls had tied 'congratulations' balloons to my desk, which was very kind, and I spent most of the morning talking about the swim to different people and being congratulated. When I finally did get back into the actual work, I found it hard to put my mind to it. Chasing up on orders and making calls to buyers put a bit of a dampener on the feeling I had wanted to last for ever. But I felt I had achieved something memorable in my life which could never be taken away.

Over the next few weeks I found it tough – everything went back to normal everyday life and I felt like something was missing. The swim had got under my skin and the daily discipline of pushing myself to achieve a big goal was now gone and I missed it.

By the time a few months had passed, it almost felt like it had never happened at all. There was a big gap to fill . . . again! The swim had changed me. I had thought I could put it to rest and get on with my career but I just couldn't. It was more than a swim: it had changed me for ever. I felt alive when I was training and now I felt lost without it.

Apart from my shoulder, the rest of my body had physically recovered well. I was lucky my shoulder had managed to make it that far after eighteen months of training and then swimming across the English Channel, but it was only a matter of time before something serious would happen if I continued to ignore it. My only option was to contact a shoulder specialist to arrange for an MRI scan and to find out exactly what was wrong with it.

I had private healthcare through work so I managed to get an appointment quickly. The scan showed no issue, which seemed very odd as I knew there was an obvious problem. The surgeon suggested I could have stretched the tendons, which the scan might not see. He advised me to build up the muscles in the back of the shoulders in order make the shoulder more stable, as I had a lot of movement there.

I did what he said and spent the next year trying to build the muscles up. I also limited my swimming. Every time I swam I would get a pain at the top of the shoulder that continued down the front of my arm and felt really tender. It was difficult to motivate myself to churn out the miles when I felt, with every arm stroke, that I was damaging myself further. After twelve months of no improvement, I contacted the surgeon again and he suggested surgery as an option.

I was going through a bad period in my work life. I had left the job at Russell Hobbs for a promotion with a packaging company but was made redundant within nine months due to the company's financial difficulties. It seemed the best time to have my shoulder operated on.

What the surgeon discovered was more severe than he had envisaged. In the year following my swim, the long head of the biceps tendon connecting the upper end of the biceps muscle to the bone had partially ruptured and attached itself to the supraspinatus tendon at the back of the shoulder. This would explain the painful tightness I experienced: even to just raise my arm to shoulder height would hurt. It seems from the surgeon's explanation that my shoulder had most likely been damaged prior to swimming the English Channel, and therefore I had completed the swim with the short head of the biceps tendon the weaker of the two that holds the muscles together. I thought it hurt a little! During the operation he attached it back, but he wasn't able to unstick the tendons.

After this first operation, the surgeon asked me, 'Do you ever want to swim again?'

'Yes,' I said. 'I want to swim from Spain to Morocco.'

He replied, 'When I said "swim again", I meant for leisure!'

I had been thinking for a while that it would be a good challenge to do Europe to Africa. I hadn't said anything to anyone as I wanted to get my shoulder fixed first and give myself a fighting chance.

The surgeon laughed and said, 'In that case we will have to look at it again in eight weeks and see if it has healed.'

I could tell he thought I had very little chance of swimming it.

I had six weeks in a sling with a rolled-up towel under my arm and was not allowed to extend or move it from that position. After that time, I was able to mobilise it for two weeks before he operated for a second time.

The operation was supposed to be a quick look to see that the attachment had healed; it was scheduled to take no longer than forty-five minutes. Whilst I was under anaesthetic, the tendon tore further and had to be repaired. In total, the operation took almost three hours.

Afterwards, the surgeon didn't fill me with too much confidence when he said, 'Hopefully, with all the shoulder rotations you will do in swimming, it will unstick itself.' He indicated to me that the shoulder was not really in any shape to do a marathon swim; it was approximately 60–70 per cent fit and we were also relying on the reattachment of the tendon holding; there was no guarantee, after thousands of overarm shoulder rotations, that this would be the case.

After the second operation I had a further six weeks in a sling. It was not a great time for me, having to be driven to job interviews by my parents, and I tried to focus on staying fit even though my arm was in a sling. I would go to the gym and train on the exercise bike. I would try to conceal my arm in the hope that the staff wouldn't see my issue and not allow me to work out. This really helped me mentally, giving me an outlet and release from the negativity in my work life, and continued to provide some structure and balance. I am not good just sitting at home.

I had a follow-up appointment with the surgeon to find out how the operation had gone and he reported that it had been a partial success. Well, it was better than no success, but it left a doubt as to how my shoulder would cope if I carried on with open-water swimming.

I counted down the weeks until I would be able to swim again. He had advised me to do some light swimming ten to twelve weeks after the operation, and as soon as the ten weeks were up I went back into the pool. My shoulder was quite stiff and sore, so I took it very slowly for the first few sessions.

I had at least landed a temporary job working at a charity for underprivileged children, which was completely different from what I was used to. It made me look at work a lot differently, in a positive way, as this job was giving back to the community. Unfortunately, I couldn't afford to live on the wages and I fell back into a more familiar commercial job working in a marketing company. This turned out to be a mistake and three months later I was looking for work again.

I was constantly frustrated and couldn't understand how I had got into such a mess in my work life. The thought of starting the swim training again and taking on a new challenge was the only focus that made sense, the only thing that gave me any feeling of work–life balance.

Fourteen weeks into the rehabilitation of my shoulder, Chris phoned me out of the blue one evening and said, 'Do you fancy coming to Dover Harbour with me? I need to do a training session at night.'

I'm not very good at saying no at the best of times, and when it comes to swimming I never say no. I immediately replied, 'Yeah, sure, I'll be over in thirty minutes.'

I packed my things and went over to his house. When I arrived he said, 'I was only joking.'

I couldn't believe it. Agreeing to join him hadn't been the most sensible thing to do as I had been operated on only fourteen weeks previously, but I just hadn't wanted to let him down. I said, 'Well, I'm here now – what do you want to do?'

'OK,' he said. 'Let's go.'

It was 9 p.m. and it would take at least three and a half hours to get there. It seemed crazy if he wasn't bothered about going and I was only doing it to support him, but we went anyway and arrived at the coast around half past midnight. After getting an hour or so's sleep in the car at some nearby services, we headed over to the swim spot we'd trained at before the Channel swim, arriving at 2.15 a.m. Now that I was there it was quite exciting, in a strange way, as well as being a crazy idea. It made me feel happy that I would be reacquainted with the open water after well over a year of not going in. The thought of swimming in pitch-black added to the excitement. It had really been tough not swimming for so long and I felt like a piece of me had been missing.

A night security guard who was patrolling the area suddenly appeared with a torch. It was the annual regatta weekend once again. We started to get changed into our swimming trunks and he said, 'What are you doing?'

I replied, 'Going for a swim.'

He said, 'You're joking!'

'No,' I said. 'We are training and need to get some night-swimming in.'

He looked at us both as if we were mad. We had light sticks attached to our trunks for visibility and I said to him, 'If you don't see a light flashing then you know something's up.' It was meant as a joke, but he responded with, 'Nothing to do with me!'

We were making our way down over the rocky beach in the dark when I had a sudden thought: having left our clothes in the car and locked it, where was Chris thinking of putting his car keys while we swam? To this he replied, 'I'll tie them to my trunks.' I remember thinking to myself, 'Isn't it central locking? Won't water damage the battery?' But I said nothing and my mind switched back to thinking about the swim and how my shoulder would fare. I walked into the water and instantly felt happy to be back where I belonged.

I didn't know how long I could comfortably swim for with the shoulder, but my plan had been to do a couple of hours until the sun came up. Given that it was only 2.30 a.m., a couple of hours were never going to take me through to sunrise, and I decided to stay out there for as long as Chris wanted to, if I was able. I didn't want to leave him out there in the dark by himself in case there was any issue. Training in the dark brings with it added hazards, especially in the sea. Having someone spotting from shore would have been preferable, just in case one or both of us came into difficulty. There are now organised night swims, which are not only great fun, but a much safer way to practice.

It dawned on me how much I had missed swimming in open water. Swimming in the dark is a good mental challenge it adds another dimension when you can barely see in front of you. The only lights that guided us were those of the buildings running parallel to the harbour. It was quite disorientating and after a short while, even though the water was flat-calm, I started to be sick. I couldn't believe it. I was shaking my head in confusion as to why this would happen. Chris started to laugh, although it backfired on him: hearing me vomit made him retch and be sick.

After this embarrassment was over, I felt a lot better. My shoulder was stiff throughout, but really started to get sore at the two-hour mark. It was still dark, as expected, so I carried on. At three hours fifteen minutes, I felt that I needed to rest my shoulder, the light had started to come up so I felt happier leaving Chris to cover a few more hours by himself. He untied his car keys from his swim shorts and passed them to me. I walked up the bank and pressed the button to unlock the car. As predicted, the door wouldn't open. What made matters worse was that it was now starting to rain, so the air temperature wasn't great.

I turned the key in the lock, which opened the door but immediately set the alarm off. I put the key in the ignition and the alarm was still going off. I grabbed my change of clothes and locked the door, as it was the only way I could switch the alarm off and not wake all of Dover up. I waved at Chris to come out of the water.

'I can't get in,' I told him. 'The fob doesn't work! I need to ring roadside assistance.' Chris replied, 'I'm not a member of roadside assistance.'

Fortunately I was and so I rang them myself, resisting the temptation to kill him. When I got through, I told them the embarrassing situation we were in: that a friend of mine had tied the keys to his trunks and gone swimming in the sea, and now the battery wouldn't work. The cavalry arrived and I'm not sure how he kept a straight face.

I said, 'I bet you've never been called out for something like this before?'

'You would be surprised at what we are called out for,' he replied.

By this time there were other swimmers who had turned up for training that morning and they thought it was hilarious. We looked a couple of idiots.

The swim had served its purpose: it got my competitive juices flowing again and I thought more seriously about the Gibraltar Strait swim that I had mentioned to the surgeon. I liked the sound of this swim as it would be a good challenge, swimming from Tarifa to Tangier, Europe to Africa. The swim has very strong currents, high winds, big swells and the temperature fluctuates from 21 degrees to 15 degrees where the Mediterranean meets the Atlantic in the middle of the Strait.

I spoke to Chris about my intention to swim it and persuaded him to join me. The swim is around 10 miles long, which is half the distance of the English Channel. Something in my head was telling me it wasn't enough of a challenge and that I had to consider a return trip. Only five people had ever swum there and back before, none of them British, so as well as being a major challenge it also presented an opportunity to be the first British person to achieve a two-way, which tugged at my competitive nature. The strait is home to a large variety of marine species including pilot whales and bottlenose dolphins. I have always been very passionate about marine life and thought it would be very apt to raise money for the Whale and Dolphin Conservation (WDC).

I contacted Rafael, president of the Gibraltar Strait Swimming Association, to tell him our intentions. He tried to put me off the idea, telling me we would have to cross in three and a half hours, the British one-way record at the time, in order to swim back. You are pushed for time and as there are only eight miles of coastline, if you are not far enough back to Tarifa, the current could sweep you out to the Atlantic Ocean. As water flows in and out of the Mediterranean, there are two currents that are formed. An upper layer of Atlantic water flows eastward into the sea, over a lower layer of Mediterranean water flowing westward into the ocean. This is known as the Mediterranean outflow water.

Rafael said we would have to swim 4 kilometres an hour throughout, minimum, to stand any chance of completing it. Great, a target!

As I began training for the swim, my shoulder continued to be sore and my concern was that, if I swam the way I did for the English Channel, I might not have a shoulder left. I had ignored injuries in the past and was at risk of proving Einstein's definition of insanity: 'doing the same thing over and over again and expecting different results'. I realised that this time I had to do something about it and change the way I swam.

A friend recommended a local swim instructor and I had a couple of lessons. I hadn't been coached before and it made me think about the front crawl differently as the technique he taught focused on rotation. It's a concept that has been a talking point in swimming for a number of years, with different theories as to why and how the rotation should be carried out to benefit the swimmer. For example, some coaches will talk about a body roll, which involves shoulder, torso and hip together. I personally needed to offload pressure from the left shoulder and be as delicate as I could on hand entry and extension, so as not to cause irritation to the shoulder.

I thought about the core and how it powers the whole motion for so many sports, including golf, boxing, cricket and shot-put, and I looked at sports and activities with very similar actions to swimming, such as kayaking. The core is a muscle group with the fastest, most efficient way to propel yourself into a movement, maximising power and saving energy. Therefore, if the core rotates the torso instead of the other way around, it will take pressure off shoulders, wrists and elbows. This is exactly what I needed to do – I just had to find a way to make it work for swimming.

I practised completely relaxing the front arm as it entered the water and using the pulling arm to guide it into extension.

Doing this didn't aggravate the shoulder, and incredibly I seemed to glide further and save energy if I was in the right position. I wondered whether this was as a result of the chest muscles on the extended arm being completely relaxed.

The rotation was also a revelation. Getting as close as possible to a full 90 degrees from side to side created a maximum force to power me forward, as long as I started the motion by turning the core muscle (top oblique) first, before pulling with the arms and shoulders. To rotate over 90 degrees didn't work as it instigated my chest muscles, while under 90 degrees gave me less power and less forward motion.

It was then down to timing and the position of my head and front arm, which needed to be deep in order to create the optimum streamlined body position with my hip up. By swimming hip to hip, I had less body mass going through the water, which proved to be more efficient as there was less drag.

All these findings were so exciting, though I wasn't sure how they would affect my speed; this swim across the Gibraltar Strait was all about how fast I could go.

I didn't have long to make these changes to my stroke; although the principles were there, I wasn't confident that I could put them all into action in such a short period of time, let alone with speed.

14

SWIM #2 GIBRALTAR STRAIT – SWIMMING BOTH WAYS SEEMED A GOOD IDEA!

At the end of June, Chris and I travelled to Tarifa, the starting point for our swim across the Gibraltar Strait. The odds were a little stacked against us making the two-way, but we had to believe it was possible. I knew we would need to be at our best to stand a chance, and we needed the weather to be kind to us.

We met up with Rafael a couple of days after arriving and he said, 'You will need to be across one way and three quarters back by seven hours thirty minutes, otherwise you won't have a chance of making it due to the current.'

We accepted this and I discussed with Chris that we couldn't even think in terms of swimming both ways: we just needed to focus on going one way, and only then should we think about making it back.

Every day we would do forty-five minutes to an hour in a bay, hoping we could go the next day, and each time the weather let us down and Rafael would call and advise that it was too windy. I knew this waiting game all too well from the English Channel, but that didn't make it any easier. After eight days we still hadn't gone and we both had a plane ticket home in two days' time. We started working out if our places of work would let us have any more time off and if we should get another flight ticket.

We stayed with our families in what can only be described as two large huts. They were situated on a farm with little wind protection. The wind was so strong on some of the nights that the buildings shook and felt like they were going to collapse.

Finally, on the ninth and last possible day, we received a call from Rafael around 8 a.m., saying the conditions were good to swim and that we should start at 11 a.m. It was a shame for Chris's girlfriend, Angela, as she had had to go home a couple of days earlier due to work.

We arrived early at the harbour with my parents, who had arrived a few days earlier to give us a send-off, and Gareth, an old neighbour and friend of theirs who now lived in Spain, came along as well. I was a little nervous, but they were good nerves. We knew our strategy was to swim as fast as we could one way and not even think about the way back. It was important we stuck together and worked as a team, for safety reasons. I had more speed than Chris, but I knew he would give it his best.

We were due to leave the harbour at 9 a.m. Rafael had expressed the need to leave on time as we could be affected by the current later on in the swim, so every minute counted. But at 9 a.m. there was no sign of the pilot. It wasn't until 9.20 a.m. that they turned up, which made me a little nervous. There were two boats, a RIB and a fishing boat that would go up ahead and track the best route with GPS. The RIB would be alongside us at all times. This was different from the English Channel, which is normally just one large boat. As the RIB was close to the water, it would make it easier to distribute the energy drinks. It would also be great for morale to be able to hear any clapping or shouting from our crew.

At 9.30 a.m., after a five-minute boat ride, we arrived at the starting point, which was a bunch of rocks in Tarifa next to the lighthouse. The plan was to touch them and the swim would then start. Unlike the English Channel, where you have to leave the water to begin, it is too dangerous to exit here and touching the rock is acceptable. Otherwise the rules of swimming the Gibraltar Strait are the same as for the English Channel: you can't wear a wetsuit – normal swim trunks and hat only – and you can't touch the boat.

As soon as we'd touched the rocks we started sprinting as if it were a 100-metre race. I took the decision to lead the way; Chris is competitive like me and I knew he wouldn't want to be left behind and that it would get the best out of him.

We came in on the first hour for a feed and had made some significant ground. On the second hour, I saw an adult and baby dolphin swimming underneath us and I could hear pilot whales doing pulsed calls to each other. I stopped once to look but was anxious to keep moving due to the time constraints we were under.

The conditions were in our favour, though; the water was fairly flat and certainly better than during my English Channel crossing, so we continued to cover good ground. Just before the second hour was up, I felt a sudden drop in water temperature, from around 21 to 15 degrees, as we went from the Mediterranean to the Atlantic side. It wasn't an issue as

I had been training in Dover in the colder temperatures – in fact, it felt quite nice.

After two hours thirty minutes, I let Chris go past me, thinking that, if he was leading, it might drive him on for the last hour. He stopped and turned to me and said, 'What's wrong? Come on, we can't hang around – we need to get moving.'

'You're joking!' I shouted. 'I've let you go past me.'

It irritated me a little and brought out my competitive side: I swam past him again. Chris and I have always been light-hearted with each other but I thought, 'What a cheek – I was doing it to help him.'

We came in for a drink at the three-hour mark. I could see Morocco, and it looked close. The pressure was now on to finish within three hours thirty minutes. We had a quick drink and set off, pushing ourselves harder than ever. I started sprinting. Before long, a wave hit me and my goggles filled with water. I knew I didn't have time to adjust them as every minute mattered. I swam with my goggles full of salty seawater, my eye stinging, in a desperate final push to finish that would give us the opportunity to turn back for the return journey.

As we got closer, I could hear the crew shouting, 'Stay to the right and touch a rock!' I was 5 metres away and wasn't sure why I couldn't just touch the rocks I was heading for, but communication out there in the ocean is very difficult at the best of times, as I had ear plugs in. I swam at a right angle to the rocks until they shouted for me to touch them. Chris ignored or didn't hear the shout and was to the left. I think they were just concerned that if we headed too far left we could potentially miss the rocks.

We touched the rocks in Tangier together in a time of three hours twenty-five minutes, breaking the British record. I hadn't planned this far ahead about what should happen next. I knew we were allowed to have ten minutes sitting on a rock, clearing the water, before turning around if we wished. Although I didn't expect a rest.

I was right in thinking that: our crew immediately starting shouting, 'Come back, come back!' I remember thinking, 'This is an expensive way to travel to Morocco.'

We pushed off the rocks in Morocco and started to make our way back to Spain. This gave me such a massive boost, as I remembered Rafael, when I first enquired about the swim, really trying to put me off attempting the two-way. 'Not only do you need fast pace,' he'd said, 'but the currents have to fall in your favour.' During the first leg the current had pushed us more to the west, and it would now be pushing us to the east on the second leg.

I knew Rafael had said it takes twice as long on the way back as the currents are much stronger, but I convinced myself that it would be different with us – we would make it back in three hours thirty minutes. I found that thinking about the best possible outcome kept my mind positive and helped drive me on.

At five hours fifty minutes we were around halfway back on the second leg and I could see we were heading in a straight line back to the nearest point in Tarifa, which was the lighthouse. It all seemed to be going great and I remember thinking, 'I don't know what Rafael was talking about – this is going to be straightforward.' Shortly after I thought that, we were waved in for a feed and the crew went from being relaxed to shouting, 'You have to swim faster.'

'Why?' I said. 'What's happened?'

'The tide is turning,' they answered. 'You have to swim faster.'

My heart rate suddenly went up by about fifty beats a minute. The pressure was now on and we had to react to it.

Chris and I had been swimming quite far apart on the way back – it was almost as if he was trying to swim off to Majorca at times. He had been told to stick close to the boat, but kept veering off. The pilot of the RIB didn't like it, from a safety viewpoint, as he had to keep leaving me by myself to tell Chris to swim closer to the boat. I didn't mind when it happened – I just wasn't sure whether I was going in the right direction. I was conscious we had been swimming more slowly on the way back as the first leg had taken a lot out of us. We had to now pick up the pace – we didn't have a choice. I increased the stroke rate, which went against what I was trying to achieve with the new stroke, but there was no thought to technique now – I just had to swim as fast as I could.

After every feed the crew would say the same: 'You've got to go faster.' At one point I shouted back in frustration, 'I can't go any faster!'

So many emotions were running through my brain. I thought, 'When am I going to get a chance to do this swim again?' How had this happened? The RIB crew continued to look anxious – I could tell from their body language. Around eight hours in I heard Chris's sister saying, 'You have two miles to go and you have thirty minutes to do it in.' I thought it was impossible but had to keep pushing, just in case. I was so upset, for I felt the chance of making it across was slipping away.

At the thirty-minute feed I shouted, 'Don't bother, there's

no point me having a drink.' I thought, 'I may as well just keep swimming until they tell me to get out.'

At forty-five minutes, the RIB came to me and my crew insisted I had a feed, then drove off to feed Chris, who was even further away now. I didn't know it at the time, but it turned out that Chris's sister had been wrong. (She could have been confused as there is a cut-off time after which it is illegal to be in the water, due to immigrants potentially trying to swim from Morocco.)

I heard the pilot say into his radio, 'Swimming man in water need more time.' Unbeknownst to me, the coastguard had agreed to an additional forty-five minutes if we needed it. As I didn't know this, I kept looking behind at the RIB, waiting for the signal to say it was over. Another thirty minutes went by and still no signal. I didn't know what was going on.

At just over nine hours thirty minutes, I saw the main boat had stopped up ahead. I thought it must be the signal that the swim was over and they were going to call me in. Then I realised next to them was a small rock. I still didn't believe it was Tarifa and completion of the swim. I swam closer and closer. I shouted, 'Is this the finish?' I couldn't hear a response apart from clapping. As I came within 10 metres of the rock, I realised it must be. My head was so confused. I started to turn around to look for Chris. The crew in the main boat and the RIB screamed at me to keep going. I wanted us to finish together but Chris was nowhere to be seen. I did as they said and swam to the rock and cleared the water in Tarifa in a time of nine hours and thirty-nine minutes. I think it was the most uncomfortable rock I have ever sat on; however, at that moment it was the best place in the world.

It was an amazing feeling to be the first British person to

swim the Gibraltar Strait both ways. I had gone through a roller coaster of emotions and couldn't believe I had made it.

I was now concerned about Chris. It would put a massive dampener on things if he didn't make it too. As I had left the water and had my finish confirmed, I was OK to turn back in search of him. Shortly afterwards he suddenly appeared and I was so relieved to see him. I swam the last 20 metres back alongside him and we both left the water together and gave each other a hug.

When we were back on the boat, it was clear we were a little shell shocked and looked like we had fought 12 rounds with a world champion boxer. It didn't matter, we had done it and were only two of eight people in the world to have completed the feat without a wetsuit. The map we were shown afterwards confirmed how the currents had started to take us after halfway, as Rafael had said they would, but due to speed and wind against the current we had managed to stay within the eight miles of coastline.

We were taken back to the harbour, and it was great to be congratulated by my mum and dad. It was a huge relief. The swim had taken a lot out of me due to the speed we had no choice but to maintain, but it gave me a huge confidence boost.

We flew back the next day and I went to my new job as a national account manager at Indesit, a white-goods manufacturer. It was such a great feeling to have accomplished another big swim and I felt invigorated, hoping this new role would keep my mind busy.

Prior to the Gibraltar Strait swim, I had committed to a two-way Windermere race with an organisation called the British Long Distance Swimming Association (BLDSA). The event takes place every two years and I quite fancied it as

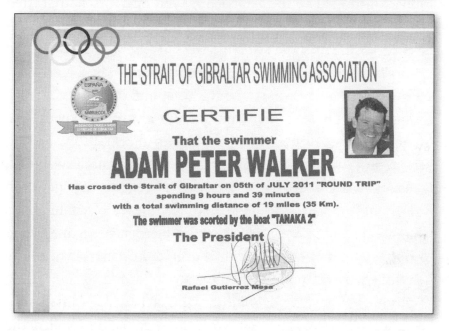

Windermere is the longest lake in the UK at 10.5 miles, so 21 miles in total, the same as the English Channel. I knew I was pushing myself as it was only five weeks after the Gibraltar Strait swim, which didn't leave me with much recovery time.

A lake posed a different challenge to swimming in the ocean. As it is fresh and not salt water, there is no buoyancy to assist body position. Windermere has a slight tide and can even be quite turbulent in significantly windy weather conditions.

I felt confident after completing my second channel swim and I thought it would be relatively straightforward. I checked into Langdale Chase Hotel located in Troutbeck, only a few minutes' drive from the start of the swim. There were no real nerves that evening and I even watched a movie until 1.30 a.m. If anything, I was too relaxed and not taking it seriously. In the morning I had to check out as there was a wedding, and I spent the day walking around the centre of Windermere with little concern about the swim.

I arrived at the lake around 6.30 p.m. The swim was scheduled for an 8 p.m. start. The reason it was at night was to avoid any boat traffic. This would be a new experience for me, as most of the swim would be in darkness. We each had to provide our own boat crew – well, when I say 'boat' I mean rowing boat! I had my wife with me to navigate as well as Jim, who had been part of the crew on my English Channel crossing, along with his friend Ellery. Jim had agreed to do the rowing, which was a challenge in itself as it would be all through the night until morning. He had the great idea of putting yellow tape around the oars so I could see them as I swam next to the boat.

The race had strict rules, based on the English Channel's. It had to be standard-size swim shorts, one swim hat and no wetsuit. At 7.45 p.m. I was changed and ready to swim, and stood there at the side of the lake thinking, 'What have I let myself in for?' The truth was, I had achieved my objective of swimming the English Channel and the two-way Gibraltar Strait, and this was not a priority. The organiser was scanning to make sure everyone was adhering to the rules of the event. She walked past me and said, 'You can't wear those shorts – they are not standard and too long.'

I said, 'They're just normal size.'

She said, 'If you win the race I can't acknowledge the swim – it won't count.'

Fortunately Chris was doing the swim too and had the same size shorts as me. I had to take them off and so did he so we could prove they were the same size. Once we did that she was happy and said it was OK for me to wear them; my swim would count.

There were around twenty experienced long-distance swimmers in the race. I looked out to the lake and thought, 'Well, no backing out now.' Not that I would have – I just wasn't feeling inspired to do the swim.

We waded into the water. It was a similar temperature to the English Channel, around 16 degrees, and the air temperature was cool as it was getting dark. We all lined up, a whistle was blown and we were off.

The adrenaline kicked in straight away and I started pushing myself hard. I wasn't sure how you race 21 miles and for a second I think my mind thought it was a short distance. I swam fast for the first hour. Chris suggested before the swim that we would swim together, but I knew I would never hear the end of it if he beat me. I was in third place and the two leaders were in sight. As I approached one hour, I had my first drink. It was the most negative I'd ever felt on a swim, and I said, 'I'm hating this!' The response back from the boat was, 'Just get on with it!'

My head was pounding and I felt really sick; I knew it couldn't have been motion sickness. I could only put it down to feeling physically tired. Perhaps I hadn't fully recovered since Gibraltar. I reached an hour and a half and sure enough I was sick. My pace slowed right down and something felt really wrong. I continued to will my arms over, but I wasn't enjoying it at all and kept stopping to adjust my goggles as they felt too tight and were giving me a headache. I just couldn't relax.

Another hour went by and it felt like a real grind. We passed one of the islands on the lake and people must have been camping there; as I swam past I saw two very drunk-looking individuals with beer cans. I was expecting some abuse yelled at me, but it was as if they had seen a ghost. I have always found people's reactions to swimming quite funny – the stares you get swimming in open water, especially when they are intoxicated!

By the time I reached three hours, I felt particularly cold. I wondered whether that was just my mind playing tricks on me, as I was only three quarters of the way across the first stretch. I later found out that a number of people had given up around three hours, including the male winner of two years earlier. I went through my mental focus techniques, visualising being warm and swimming in my warm ring, but the biggest issue was that I wasn't passionate about the swim and so my guard and focus were down. I carried on regardless as I'm too stubborn and the thought of quitting could never be an option.

I passed the four-hour mark and I knew Chris was quite far behind. I didn't know the lake that well and kept convincing myself that I was at the end when I saw moored boats, which kept me going, even though it wasn't the case. At around four hours fifty minutes I touched the end. What a relief – at least one way was done.

I was still very tired and my shoulder felt sore. I thought, 'I'm on my way home now', which was a huge mental boost. There was a big gap behind me and I wasn't going to catch the other two, who were flying off ahead, so the pressure was off – I just needed to finish. I had asked a lot of my shoulder and it was now all about preserving it. I didn't have long after Gibraltar to work on my new technique and it was still far from perfect; I was anxious not to cause too much irritation so I tried to ease off a little and just get the swim over and done with.

By the time it reached 5 a.m. the sun was starting to come up and I was nine hours in. It was stunning and that really lifted my spirits. I realised how lucky I was to be out there, after moaning to myself for much of the swim. I kept counting strokes up to sixty, then another set – anything to distract my brain. I no longer felt cold from the water temperature, which was a good lesson for me: temperature concerns can pass if you just keep going. You really have to get to know what your body can handle and you only find this out by pushing through.

As I approached ten hours I knew it had been a slower second leg, but it was just finishing that mattered and I could see cars and a crowd of people, so I knew we must be close. At ten hours thirty-one minutes I finished and walked out to a very nice round of applause. I was the third person back.

It had been far from a perfect swim. I am glad I did it, though. The lake is beautiful and it was a big lesson in not taking swims for granted – each long-distance swim has its own challenges and has to be respected in order to get the best out of you. I learned a lot from this swim and I knew it would only make me stronger as a result.

TWO WAY WINDERMERE CHAMPIONSHIP

BRITISH LONG DISTANCE SWIMMING ASSOCIATION

THE PRESIDENT & EXECUTIVE COMMITTEE
have pleasure in awarding this certificate to

Adam Walker

who completed the course on

13th - 14th August 2011

in

10 hours *31* minutes *17* seconds

President *B Thomas*

Championship Secretary *[signature]*

LAKE WINDERMERE

WATERHEAD

FELL FOOT

BOWNESS

WINDERMERE

MILES

KILOMETRES

15

OCEAN'S SEVEN – THE ULTIMATE ENDURANCE SWIMMING CHALLENGE

I now needed to keep working on the stroke if I was to take on another swim. I wasn't sure which one to do next but I knew it had to be something I was passionate about. I went on the internet looking for swims and read about a challenge devised by a man called Steve Munatones, the former USA open-water swim coach, who is well respected in the sport. The challenge was called the Ocean's Seven. Based on his vast knowledge and experience, Steve had brought together the seven toughest ocean swims in the world, selected on the basis that they showcased a wide spectrum of challenges, both physical and mental, that an ocean can throw at you, such as extreme cold water, deadly marine life, huge swells, high winds, fast currents and tides.

On the list was the English Channel and Gibraltar Strait, one way. I only had five more to go.

It was the second time in my life that it felt like a light bulb had switched on in my head; I thought, 'That's what I need to do – swim the Ocean's Seven!' I knew it would be a push to do another five swims with my shoulder and the odds were stacked against me, but I thought if I could continue to improve my stroke, then, God willing, anything was possible.

One of the swims on the list was called the Molokai Strait, which I had never heard of before. It is a 26-mile swim in Hawaii from Molokai island to Oahu island, also known as the Ka'iwi Channel swim, and it's the longest of the Ocean's Seven swims. I quickly made up my mind that this would be the next swim; Hawaiian waters were much warmer than what I was used to and, after all, it was Hawaii – what could go wrong there?

16

SWIM #3 MOLOKAI STRAIT – HAWAII! HOW HARD CAN IT BE?

As I was researching my swim across the Molokai Strait, I found out there were two pilots who could take swimmers across. The one I chose was called Jim and his main job was fishing and running kayak trips. I called him and booked the swim for the following year, in August 2012.

I did my winter pool training and worked on my technique further. The stroke was really starting to come together, taking pressure off my shoulder so it was less painful, and I was much more efficient. I was also as fast as I had ever been, maintaining times consistently over a longer distance.

I had heard that only twenty people had ever crossed the Molokai Strait due to the big swells, strong currents and deadly marine life.

My next challenge was to find the money to pay for the swim. On the last two I had managed to get the money together, but this one was much more expensive; I worked out that, with the swim cost, accommodation and flight, it was going to be in excess of £8,000. I had never seen money as a barrier and knew I would find it from somewhere – or just put it on the credit card and pay it later. I couldn't allow money to get in the way of my dreams.

I mentioned my challenge to the marketing brand manager at work, a girl called Libby, in the hope that the company would want to support me financially. She was amazing; she managed to get the company to agree to pay for two flights and the swim, which was fantastic. I agreed in return to give them as much exposure as possible. This was a real weight off my mind.

I now had just the accommodation to sort out. I wrote to forty hotels to see if they would be prepared to offer me two rooms for two weeks. (I needed two rooms as I would require another crew member to feed me from the boat.) In return I would provide exposure for the hotel with all media I received over there. The only hotel that agreed to support me was the Equus in Honolulu, a family-owned boutique hotel owned by a man called Mike Dailey, who ran the Hawaiian polo team. They even agreed to support my crew, Chris and Angela, which I was extremely grateful for.

I booked for two weeks in case the weather wasn't kind and I had to wait a while to go. My plan was to have a few days' rest while waiting for the weather conditions that would allow the swim attempt.

My wife and I arrived in Honolulu after an eighteen-hour flight and two stops, meeting up with Chris and Angela, who had travelled the week before. It was late at night and, after a pub dinner at 1 a.m., we went to sleep at 2.30 a.m. At 8 a.m. I heard the hotel phone ringing. It was the boat pilot, Jim, saying that we were to meet him at Molokai island at 3.30 a.m. the following morning. I didn't think the tide started that soon, but he said he was taking a group out kayaking in a couple of days and wouldn't be available after that, plus the weather was looking bad anyway so the best bet was tomorrow. I responded with an excited yet slightly panicked voice, 'OK, great.'

The realisation of what this actually meant suddenly hit me. I had to book flights over to the island and a hotel. I suddenly felt really disorganised. I hadn't even had a chance to get used to the time difference or have any rest at all. I rang Chris and told him the news. I then immediately went on the internet to find a flight and hotel. I managed to get the last four seats on the plane to fly out, but no one was picking up the phone at the hotel. It was the only hotel on Molokai so I hadn't any other options. I also spoke to Linda Kaiser, a Hawaiian open-water swimming legend who had helped me set up booking the swim. She was concerned that the wind was supposed to be up to 25 knots per hour, and the swimming conditions were not going to be great. She said 'Is Jim sure the conditions are going to be OK?' I wasn't sure what to do – I had little choice if the weather was going to get worse as I was there for two weeks and couldn't afford not to swim. My company definitely wouldn't pay for another flight over here. I had to go for it.

We had also not been made aware by Jim that we had to arrange our own observer – this was news to me as every other pilot sorts this out – and in the end it was agreed Chris could be the observer. This whole conversation did nothing for my nerves.

Before my trip out to Hawaii, I had been communicating with a resident ex-surfer called Wilson. He had invented a shark defence system that lets off an electrical pulse which the sharks don't like – it is not dangerous to them, just a deterrent. I thought it would be good to have some extra protection as it was the Pacific Ocean, after all – and there are various breed of sharks out there and I didn't want to be mistaken for a seal!

I told Wilson I was going that evening so he came to the hotel with the units and a colleague of his, Glenn. He explained how they operated when they touched water. The one-kilo unit went around the ankle with a Velcro strap. I had seen similar, bulkier, units before, but this was really compact and I would hardly notice it. He also agreed to loan me another three units that had been designed specifically to hang over the side of the boat. They had long leashes that released the same electrical pulse as the one around my ankle. He explained that this would increase the size of the electrical field and give me extra protection.

I continued to phone the hotel on Molokai over the next couple of hours, still with no reply, so eventually I emailed them. Finally, after a few hours, I received a reply: 'Dear Mr Walker. Apologies for the late response. I have received your request for 2 rooms, however the hotel is on fire and we will get back to you.' I started to think maybe this swim was jinxed – it took all my mental training to remain positive and stay calm.

While waiting to see if we had a hotel, I was contacted by KITV, a Hawaiian TV station. A really nice reporter called Andrew Pereira came to the Equus to interview me. The Hawaiian people know how treacherous those waters can get so they were interested in finding out more about the swim.

On the flight to Hawaii, I had watched a documentary about the canoe races that take place each year across the

Molokai Strait. They interviewed one of the competitors, who said, 'It's one of the hardest kayak races in the world, due to the big swells and currents, it's very dangerous.' They used dramatic music and slow motion to emphasise how tough it was. As I was watching I kept thinking, 'Kayaking? I have to *swim* this!'

After the interview with Andrew, I received an email from the hotel on Molokai saying the fire had stopped and although there was damage to the hotel they had reserved me two rooms. What a huge relief – I could finally start focusing on the swim. I had now just an hour and a half to switch off and rest before going to the airport. I went back to my hotel room to try to sleep. I knew I needed all the rest I could get after the long flight and that I would be swimming only twenty-four hours after arriving. It was impossible to sleep, though – my mind was spinning. I just lay there thinking about the swim and praying for a successful crossing. The time flew by and soon we were making our way to the domestic airport in Oahu to fly to the island.

As we were queuing to board the plane, the TV news broadcast my interview. It was all very real now, and I knew I had better be ready – I would need to be at my best. This would be my longest-ever unassisted swim. We flew over the body of water in the twenty-seater plane and I tried not to think about the fact that I was going to swim back!

I tried to keep my mind clear and not overanalyse it. I felt I was in a good place mentally; training had gone well and crossing three 20-mile swims had given me a lot of confidence. I thought about those successes and told myself I knew how to conquer this. I firmly believed that if I didn't make the swims difficult in my mind, they wouldn't become difficult in reality.

We arrived at the tiny Molokai airport just after 8 p.m. and took a taxi to the hotel. Molokai is a very small place, with a population of just 7,000. It didn't take long to get to the hotel and I went to bed around 9 p.m. It had all been a whirlwind since arriving in Hawaii and I needed to get my mind focused on the job in hand.

Again, I couldn't sleep. Clem had made me one of his hypnotherapy CDs to listen to. He created one specifically for every swim; they were fantastic, helping me relax and flooding my subconscious full of positive thoughts so that I could visualise my success. I also listened to inspirational music. I didn't want silence to allow my mind to drift into any negative thoughts. Long-distance ocean-swimming is very unforgiving – if you have any self-doubt, your mind will try to find a way to make those negative thoughts multiply and potentially convince you to quit. On the flip side, positivity is also contagious and you can get into a good habit of alleviating any self-doubt.

At 1.30 a.m., after very little sleep, I started to get myself ready for the swim. The taxi picked us up at 2.30 a.m. and we made the ten-minute drive to the harbour where we would meet the boat and crew. It was pitch-black and very quiet. As we boarded the boat and loaded our gear, I was trying hard not to let the nerves get to me and to stay calm.

Heading out of the harbour, I thought it wouldn't take a long time to get to the starting point. I began to get ready to swim: Vaseline under the arms and back of my neck for friction, and was ready to go. I asked Jim how long before I would be entering the water and he said we wouldn't be getting in before it got light, due to the sharks. I was a little premature getting ready, it seemed.

When I first made the decision to swim the Strait, my internet research had thrown up a page on shark attacks. One story in particular attracted my attention. Only a few years previously, an open-water swimmer had been bitten on his calf by a cookiecutter shark just two hours into the swim. The shark apparently came around again and attempted to bite his chest but missed. The calf bite resulted in him having to get out of the water while his crew held his leg together in an attempt to lessen the blood loss. After reading this article, I resolved to stop looking up details of my swims on the internet.

We ended up being on the boat for two and a half hours, for much of which Jim regaled me with every story he could think of about shark attacks in the Molokai Strait. I decided the best option for me would be to put my headphones on and listen to Clem's hypnotherapy CD, as Jim's stories were not going to benefit me just before I jumped into the water.

At 5.55 a.m., the sun began to make an appearance and we made our way to a small beach area called La'au Point, where I could clear the water and start. I pulled out my goggles and swim hat and attached the electric shark unit around my ankle, then slipped into the water. My first thoughts were how warm the water was – it must have been 23 degrees, around 7 degrees warmer than the English Channel, and I had been training in water around 15 degrees so it seemed particularly comfortable.

As I began swimming to the beach for the start, I looked into the water and there was all sorts of tropical wildlife. In the English Channel I had seen four white jellyfish and that was about it. I swam around 100 metres to clear the water and a wave hit me, knocking me over before I had even started. I raised my hands up to show I had cleared the water and signalled that I was ready to begin.

I was off on my third channel swim. It seemed to take an age to get back to the boat, and when I was around 15 metres from it, Jim started to lead the way. I wanted to get alongside the boat, but he seemed happy with me swimming behind. I wasn't used to this and I found it a little annoying as I had to keep looking up to sight and check my direction. Before I entered the water Jim had told me it was a good idea to get a fast first hour before slowing down, as the currents would be taking us out into the middle of the channel. I was conscious of this and got into a good pace and rhythm quickly. After the first thirty minutes, the wave swells started to pick up and the wind was strong. It wasn't anything I couldn't handle, though, and it didn't affect my stroke too much.

The sun was out and it felt like it was going to be a glorious day. Underwater I could see what could only be described as little bits of fluff. I remember thinking, 'They look quite cute', as they floated past me . . . and then stung me repeatedly in the face. They must have been jellyfish – immediately they weren't cute any more. I stopped for a second after being stung and felt the need to shout at the boat, 'I've just been stung!' Not that they could do anything about it.

I had my first feed on the hour and everything seemed fine. The waves were getting bigger now, although I still had a few seconds between each one, giving me time to predict when to breathe. I have always preferred rolling waves as you have a few seconds to react in comparison to constant choppy water, which is what I had in the English Channel. By the second feed I felt tired and flat, which really concerned me. 'I can't afford to be tired now,' I told myself. 'I'm barely into the swim!' I started thinking what a mistake it had been not to give myself any time to get over the flight. I was now getting what I deserved – I mean, what did I expect?

I told myself the feeling would pass, like when I felt sick in the English Channel. It was just one arm in front of the other – keep it simple, Adam. My crew gave me some flat Coke and the caffeine really picked me up. At four hours the tiredness had passed and I felt more comfortable. The waves were a few feet high, making it tough to get a rhythm, but I was now well into the middle of the channel.

A few times, at the corner of my eye, I had seen the occasional dorsal fin appear up out of the water, not far away from me, and passed them off as dolphins. I worked really hard to focus on my arm strokes and staying relaxed. I was aware of the dangerous waters I was in and didn't allow my mind to drift into thinking about sharks or other potentially deadly marine life, which were no doubt not too far away. The shark defence unit gave me some reassurance. I could feel on my ankle the electrical pulse and see a little green light flashing, which indicated it was on. There was of course no guarantee of whether it was actually working or not – I just hoped it would.

At six hours, Chris decided to jump in and swim with me for support. He was allowed to swim alongside me under the same rules as the English Channel. I was glad he did, as it was good for my morale, although I wasn't feeling too bad. Not long after Chris had entered, he began stopping periodically to look underwater. He was also wearing a shark deterrent device as a precaution. I thought, 'What is he looking at?' The first thing that came into my head was that he'd seen a shark. I didn't communicate with him at the time, but he told me afterwards it was a shark around six feet in length.

I continued to take a mixture of carb drink and flat Coke. The water was really salty and I had swallowed some a few times, which made me sick. I was a professional at vomiting on swims now so it didn't faze me – I just carried on.

After eight hours twenty minutes, I looked down at my shark unit and saw the green light had turned red, which meant it had run out of charge. The boat was 20 metres in front of me and I shouted for them to come back so I could swap it for another one. They struggled to hear me at first and I had to shout a few times before they realised what I was saying and stopped. I continued to be frustrated at looking up to locate the boat; it was hurting my neck and using up unnecessary energy. I kept quiet, though, and continued on; I wanted to stay as relaxed as possible and moaning wouldn't serve any positive purpose.

I caught up with the boat and threw the old unit to Chris. The new fully charged one was passed to me on a pole. I remember Wilson saying the unit activated when it hit water, so I held it at the sides to try to avoid the electrical field. I tried to put it on out of the water by sticking my leg up as far as it would go while treading water in some kind of strange synchro manoeuvre. I must have looked very strange to those watching, especially as my flexibility wouldn't allow it, and in the end I was forced to put it on in the water. In doing so, I touched it where the electrical pulse was coming out and electrocuted myself with up to 200 volts. My whole body was shaking and my crew started shouting, 'Are you OK?'

'Aaah, aaah,' I responded. 'Giiive meee a minuuute . . .'

There was no easy way of attaching it without being shocked. I had stuck it on loosely with the Velcro and it was sliding around my ankle, but I didn't care – I couldn't take any more shocks. On a positive note, they really woke me up and I was raring to go.

When I came in for another drink at nine hours, I could hear the pilot say on his radio, 'He's going to break the world record!' The record was just over twelve hours and I could clearly see land. I was thinking to myself, I'm going to finish the swim within eleven and a half hours. After hearing this, I was really excited and picked up my pace. I felt relaxed, like the pressure was off and I was going to finish the swim with no issues at all. I couldn't believe how straightforward it had been and I started powering forward.

After an hour, I lifted my head up expecting to be really close to the finish. This wasn't the case. It looked like I hadn't moved forward at all. The shore must have been further away than it appeared. I continued for another hour and looked up again – I now seemed further away than I had been a couple of hours ago, and the cliffs we had been aiming for were more to the east. I still didn't say anything and kept swimming, but after the third hour I knew something wasn't right. I was now twelve hours in and I should have finished.

I shouted to the boat, 'What's happening?' and Chris replied, 'The tide has been pushing you back but don't worry, it's changing and is now with you.'

I didn't know whether to believe him or not. Either way, there was no point in me getting irritated – I had to stay focused and accept there could be another couple of hours' swimming. I changed my mindset to think of this as a positive: I had never swum for this long before.

I don't think Chris knew what the tide was going to do; he was just trying to keep me in good spirits. He explained and pointed out to me that we were going to head down the coast to a place called Portlock, which was three miles west of Sandy Beach, the nearest finish point. The boat was directing me parallel to the coast but didn't seem to be getting any closer to Portlock.

The sun was going down by now and I remembered what Jim had said about starting in daylight due to the sharks being nocturnal. I knew we were going to finish in the dark. I continued to remain calm and embrace the challenge. As darkness came upon us, it was over thirteen hours since I had started swimming. My crew passed me some new goggles with a small light attached to them. I also had a light stick attached to my swim shorts with a safety pin from the start of the swim but I didn't want to turn it on as I was conscious of attracting the sharks.

I had a kayaker on board ready to come in – he was on standby in case I was still in the water after dark. The sun went down fast and he appeared in the water next to me, which was great as I no longer had to look up and sight to see where the boat was.

The kayaker had not been in long when suddenly, with no warning, I felt like I had been slashed across the stomach with a knife. I nearly shot out of the water. I felt an instant red-hot burning feeling across my torso and inside my leg. I started to shout in agony. I am normally good at masking pain during my swims, firstly because I don't want to give it any power over me, but also because I'm conscious of not giving the boat pilot an excuse to finish the swim early. This time was different. I couldn't help it – the pain had taken hold of me.

I couldn't see anything due to the darkness. I just knew I was in a lot of trouble. The pain was not like a jellyfish sting; it was a cross between being electrocuted and slashed. I was on fire – the sort of pain your brain struggles to tolerate and is desperate to stop.

The kayaker said, in a panicked voice, 'It's either a box jellyfish or Portuguese man o' war. If you start to labour breathe or hallucinate I'm going to have to get you out.'

I monitored my breathing and thought, 'I'm labour breathing now, but I have swum thirteen and a half hours so wouldn't be able to tell the difference.' I touched my stomach and found something was stuck to me. It was tentacles.

The swim was over – well, that was my brain's instant reaction to the situation. The thought flooded my mind and there was no room for anything else. I had trained myself to cope with many obstacles in open water, from cold temperature to tiredness, sickness and stomach ache, but you can't replicate this type of pain in training and you wouldn't want to. I was upset and panicking at the same time, at the thought of the dream slipping away. I knew I would struggle to afford to do this again, so I had to find a way to carry on. I attempted to regain my composure and remember how much I wanted to conquer the swim, but it was hard to think of anything else other than the pain.

I decided to make a deal with myself to swim just one more minute. I had applied this many times in training as incentives to continue. For instance, if I was feeling the temperature, I would say, 'Just thirty more minutes, Adam, and then you can get out.' Once I achieved that, I would persuade myself to do another thirty minutes, then another, until the five- or six-hour session was done. The disappointment I would feel if I gave up was always much worse than any pain.

The situation I found myself in now was far more extreme, however. I was in agony and a big part of my brain was desperate for it to end. I had faced these dark thoughts before and found a way through them. I would see them as the devil on my shoulder trying to tell me, 'You're in too much pain. Get us out of here – you can't continue!' But on the other shoulder is an angel, and she was saying, 'Remember how much you want this . . . Don't give up – don't you dare give up!' At this point the devil was much bigger and more vocal than the angel, but the will to succeed was hanging in there and trying to become bigger and more dominant.

I had previously programmed my mind to think about my swims in a way Clem had taught me; he would say, 'Each swim is a means to an end and not the big thing – it is part of a process.' I taught myself to focus on the positives, the end goal and not the moment. But right now it was such a shock to the system that I found it too hard to focus.

The issue was that I couldn't even flatten out in the water as the pain was so intense. My legs dangled straight down towards the seabed. I asked the kayaker how long there was to go.

His reply: 'Oh, dude, it's about an hour.'

I tried to swim for one minute without stopping and I couldn't do it. I stopped again for a moment to get my thoughts together. I then tried to drag my body and swam for a few seconds and stopped again. The boat came towards me and passed me down an antihistamine pill. I then started to vomit, which lasted for a few minutes. I didn't know what was happening to me. I asked to be given a minute and the boat kept drifting forwards, waiting for my next move. The kayaker was alongside me and said it was a good thing to get the poison out of my system.

Once I felt like the vomiting had stopped, I made another

deal with myself: if I could swim past the boat, it would be like a checkpoint and I couldn't stop until the finish. The boat was 15 or 20 metres away, and once I composed myself from being sick I dragged my torso forward, still unable to lift my legs up, and with every stroke having to touch my stomach for comfort from the burning.

As I did this I started to feel very strange, like my chest was tightening up; I felt my spine tingling and then it went numb. I found out later that it was almost certainly a man o' war, and that they have 75 per cent of the toxins of a cobra snake. They pierce thousands of barbs into you – these barbs can be deadly and shut down a human being's organs, resulting in anaphylactic shock and death. Up to now on these swims I had visualised positive images and success. The image I had in my mind now was me paralysed on the boat. I tried to joke it off and said to myself, 'If you're going to paralyse me, at least let me finish this swim!' It was hard to joke about this very serious situation.

I managed to drag myself level with the boat and when I made it I forced my legs up and did a fake smile to hide the pain and deflect how I was really feeling. I suddenly felt a big shiver down my spine. I'm sure the pilot thought I was going to give up and for once in my life I felt really proud of myself as I was going to continue when it looked like there was no hope of finishing.

I'm normally so hard on myself, never truly satisfied in anything that I do, analysing my performance and thinking how I could have done better, always striving to improve. This was different and looked like a lost cause, but I wasn't going to quit. This was part of the challenge, a test of how much I wanted to complete the swim and how capable I really was. I felt like maybe this situation was supposed to happen, to prove I was truly worthy of conquering this swim and indeed the Ocean's Seven. When I was training for the English Channel, the question of how I thought I was capable of swimming all day with a bad shoulder and no previous experience had crossed my mind a few times. I would then switch the thought by thinking, 'It's just one arm in front of the other . . .'

This was the same and in order to push through and keep going, I thought, 'No other swim will ever be as bad as this and if you can conquer it, you can conquer anything.' The little talks to myself seemed to be working and spurred me on.

I sensed from the worry in the kayaker's voice that he thought the swim was finished. I knew I had an acceptable excuse to get out if I wanted to, but I definitely didn't want to. Up to this point, nothing had really affected me in this swim. Of course, it was tough and I had swum further than I had ever done before, which drove me on even when I was pushed backwards for a number of hours. But I still felt I had controlled the swim up to now. In one moment it had been turned on its head, but it was still up to me to say what happened next. I tried to not think too far ahead and to concentrate hard on shutting out the pain. It was impossible to block it out completely. I focused on positive thoughts and how much the swim meant to me. I could only hold the thought for a couple of seconds before the pain once again dominated my mind and body. I knew it was going to take every bit of mental power to block it out. I started swimming in two-minute bursts, counting strokes, saying over and over again, 'Pain lasts for a minute, success lasts for a lifetime.' The issue was that I couldn't stop touching my stomach due to the burning. It gave me a little comfort but it also slowed me down.

I went back to thinking about when I had swum the English Channel, telling myself, 'If the boat wasn't there I would make it. I haven't a choice. It's only an hour – I can handle an hour of pain.' I also didn't want to be reminded every day of giving up, of the pain being victorious over me. My brother Mark said to me after one of my channel crossings, 'My fear for you is if you don't make a swim, what it will do to you.' I had immediately shot back, 'Don't worry because I *will* make them, so you don't need to be concerned.' If I had been incapacitated and it was physically impossible for me to carry on, I would have had to accept it, but right now I could still move, albeit with horrific pain. As long as I could still swim, I had to keep doing one arm and then the other.

Another technique I used to deflect the pain was to recite in my head inspirational movie lines by the likes of Al Pacino or Sly Stallone. My favourite quote from *Rocky* is 'It ain't about how hard you hit. It's about how hard you can get hit and keep moving forward . . . That's how winning is done!' This one in particular went round and round in my head. I also turned back to *On a Clear Day*, when Frank is in the middle of the English Channel and his friend says, 'You don't have a choice – you never did!' I had said this to myself on several occasions during my swims and it had always reminded me of how much I wanted to complete them.

I would use anything I could mentally grab hold of in my mind for a few seconds to keep me moving forwards and shut out the burning. I even visualised the burning as a warm ring: whilst I had it I couldn't be cold or have hypothermia. I started shaking as I swam from the effect the sting was having on my body. I couldn't keep my head in the same place – it was twitching from side to side with the pain. I would say to myself, 'I'm so lucky . . . I'm so lucky to have this!' I tried any desperate attempt to keep going.

As I swam on, I managed to complete what was probably twenty minutes, though it seemed like for ever. I asked the kayaker how long to go and he said, 'About twenty minutes.'

I asked, 'Are we making any headway?'

'Slowly,' he replied, 'but we are.'

I wasn't sure whether he was telling me the truth or trying to keep my spirits up. Every time I looked up we seemed to be moving sideways with the current and were no closer to shore. I made another deal with myself: as long as he gave me some hope that we were making progress, I would continue. I kept asking him, with ever more frequency, how long to go, and he kept telling me twenty minutes. I didn't complain – I would just thank him and carry on. I was determined not to moan and to save as much energy as possible.

I reached an hour and was convinced we must be there, but sadly the reality was that there was a lot more swimming to go. I still couldn't see land close enough. I had battled too hard to give in now and believed the swim would finish soon. I could hardly pick up my arms. I was exhausted physically and mentally.

What I didn't realise was that the pilot was off course once he passed Sandy Beach. At this point we were past Portlock and Linda was speaking with Jim on the phone trying to get him to land near the Kahala Hotel further down. She walked along the entire beach with Wilson and Glenn, looking for us. Seeing the lights from the boat, she realised we were outside the reef and couldn't get in. Jim told her that he was going

Above: A young Adam posing for a photo with Margaret (mother), Mark (brother) and Peter (father).

Below: Adam enjoying the ocean while on holiday with his family.

Above: Adam leading the way in a rugby training session at school.

Below: The Walker family playing together in a cricket match in Spain. Left to right: brothers Mark and Kevin, father Peter and Adam, August 1996.

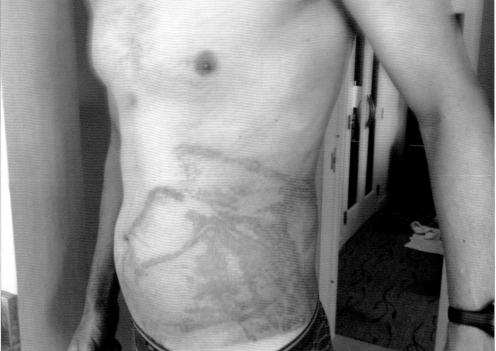

Above: Adam looking out to sea, contemplating swimming the North Channel, August 2014.

Above: The Portuguese man o' war sting Adam endured during the Molokai Channel swim, June 2012: 'these barbs can be deadly and shut down a human being's organs.'

Climbing out of the water with relief after completing the Catalina Channel swim with one functioning arm, October 2012.

Above: Being fed off the boat by girlfriend Gemma Clarke while friend John Raynor gives support, Tsugaru Strait, August 2013.

Below: A great shot of two dolphins pictured with Adam while filming for the documentary *Conversations With Dolphins* in Kaikoura, New Zealand, April 2015 (*Fiona Wardle*).

Above: Adam showcasing his unique 'Ocean Walker' technique in Wanaka, New Zealand, January 2014 (*Sandy Greenway*).

Below: Team photo with friend John and girlfriend Gemma just after Adam completed the Tsugaru Channel, August 2013.

Chris congratulating a very tired Adam on the beach at Wissant, France, after swimming the English Channel, July 2008.

Above: Adam playing ball with his two dogs, Booie (black Newfoundland) and Lady (golden retriever) at the beach in Norfolk, 2014.

Below: Coaching session with Adam at Lake Windermere practising the Ocean Walker technique, June 2015.

to land at Diamond Head Beach, which Linda thought was a bad idea as it was a very big beach with no car access – she would never find me. In the end she suggested Diamond Head Lighthouse, which was a little further on but had better access; she would have her car lights on, shining into the water, so Jim could track towards the shore.

Chris tried to help with a piece of cardboard and a pencil at one point by trying to work out where we were in the ocean using the map, as Jim said his three navigation systems were down.

It was very slow going and after another forty-five minutes of battling the current, the kayaker told me there were just five minutes to go. I thought, 'Oh my God – I'm going to make it! The pressure is off. I'm going to do it!' I swam on, counting lots of sixty strokes and the time down in my mind.

After ten minutes I thought I saw a beach and tried to put my feet down, searching for solid ground. I couldn't stand up, though – I tried again and still no sand under my feet. I looked to the side of me and knew then that it wasn't the finish. The boat was still next to me and there was no beach. I was devastated. It was so demoralising. I wondered why the kayaker had told me I had five minutes to go, but I had no energy to debate it and just kept swimming.

I was still coming in for my energy drink every thirty minutes, but it became a little pointless as I wasn't taking any in, just squirting it into my mouth and spitting it out. Finally I came in and my crew shouted, 'Last feed!' and I knew I would be finishing within thirty minutes. It was like music to my ears. I so badly wanted the swim to end and I started counting down the time in my head.

I reached thirty minutes and I still hadn't finished. It had happened again! I was waved in for another drink. I was really irritated – I had been told twice I was going to finish and still nothing. They shouted at me again to come in and I said, 'Forget it – I'm not swimming over to you.' The boat was 25 metres away and I wasn't going to waste energy swimming over, so I ignored the shouts and carried on.

I know it wasn't their fault and that they too had assumed I would have finished by now. The reason I hadn't was because of how tough it was at the end with the current still working against me. But there is nothing worse than being told you're going to finish and then not doing so. I had experienced this in the English Channel too. Right now I didn't know what was going on and it felt like the swim was never going to end.

The kayaker once again told me I had twenty minutes to go, and as it turned out on this occasion it was around that long until I saw a beach again. I had to look a few times as I didn't know whether it was real or what to believe any more. I questioned myself – maybe I was seeing things out of desperation and going delirious. I looked for a second time: it was definitely a beach.

The kayaker shouted over, 'Follow me.' Rather than straight ahead he was going sideways. This confused me more and I shouted, 'But the beach is there!'

He responded, 'It's too dangerous.'

'OK,' I said, but I ignored him and went for the shortest route forward. I was worried about being swept down the coast and missing the beach.

I trusted the kayaker, he had navigated me through the current successfully and without his and Linda's support I could have still been out there for days. The reason he wanted me to follow him was because I was surrounded by sharp rocks. But I didn't care how dangerous it was – I wasn't swimming one more metre than I had to!

I was faced with rocks protruding upwards everywhere and as I swam up to the first one I caught my arm and chest. I decided to take my goggles off to work out how to get across and stood up. As I stood up, the light attached to my goggles flew off my head and I recalled Chris joking earlier in the day, 'Make sure you don't lose the light!' I'm sure he wouldn't have minded me losing it but I would have felt bad, so I started feeling around with my foot for it. I looked back and the boat had turned around; I thought they must be going back to the harbour. There was also no sign of the kayaker either. It was all very strange as I was now alone. I picked the light up with my foot and climbed over the rocks, cutting my leg in the process. I scrambled out onto the beach in a time of seventeen hours and two minutes in total disbelief. I had done it.

There was a lady standing on the beach, I didn't know who she was but I was so glad to see her smiling face and I said to her, 'Well, that was fun!' She put a garland of flowers around my neck and gave me a big hug – it was Linda. She made a phone call to the crew and I heard her say, 'He's out and he's talking – he doesn't need an ambulance.' The boat and kayaker had left when Linda had confirmed she could see me. I was so grateful to her for her support. I wouldn't have made it without her.

Ka'iwi Channel Swim

Moloka'i to O'ahu

26 miles

Official Finisher
KA'IWI CHANNEL SWIMMERS ASSOCIATION

MOLOKA'I

O'AHU

Name: MR. ADAM WALKER

Start: Date: 06/24/2012 Time: 5:55 AM Location: LA'AU POINT

Finish: Date: 06/24/2012 Time: 22:57 PM Location: Diamond Head lighthouse

17:02

'A'OHE PU'U KI'EKI'E KE HO'A'O 'IA E PI'I

As I walked up the beach, my friends Wilson and Glenn gave me a hug and we took some photos. I also had a TV camera fixed on me from a Hawaiian TV station, though they didn't say a word. I thought I had better say something inspirational, which was a bit of an issue as I was struggling to speak with all the ulcers in my mouth caused by the salt water. The only words I could think of were those I had been repeating over and over in my head to get me through after the sting: 'Pain lasts for a minute, success lasts for a lifetime.' Although it didn't quite come out like that as I struggled to pronounce my words.

After a few photos, Wilson and Glenn took me in their car to the harbour. I had no clothes to change into and was just in my swimming trunks. I felt really bad as I had blood dripping from my leg and was drenching the car seats, but Wilson didn't care. I love Hawaiian people – they are so laid-back and extremely caring.

I met up with my crew and I gave the kayaker a hug. I felt like I owed him a lot; without his expert navigation through the current, I'm not sure I would have finished. He said, 'You are one seriously tough guy, dude. Man, you scared me out there – I thought you were a goner! I'm glad you had that shark defence unit on – did you see the shark surfing on the wave when you were finishing?'

I told him the shark unit hadn't been working for the last hour as the battery had run out, and I had been bleeding from cutting my leg on a rock. He said, 'Dude, you were really lucky.'

There was nothing about that day that made me feel I was lucky, but I took his point.

We made our way back to the Equus hotel and I was greeted

with such a warm reception by the manager, René. They even made me a plaque to congratulate me, which was very sweet.

My stomach was still on fire and I was desperate to try and ease the pain. I didn't at the time know what it was that had stung me, although the assumption was still a Portuguese man o' war. I didn't have the energy to look up on the internet how to treat such wounds, but I thought a warm shower might help. I was right – it did seem to ease the pain. My stomach was lacerated with scars where I had been stung and you could see them around my side and back. I had two long scars at the front where I had pulled the tentacles off and a twelve-inch scar inside my leg, which fortunately missed my vitals! I was a mess. It looked as bad as it felt.

I was excited to tell my parents the news. With all the issues in the last few hours, they hadn't been updated and I wasn't sure if they knew I had completed it. I sat down in the shower on the phone with the warm water pounding down on me and told my parents. My mum was very relieved to hear from me. She worries a lot and was convinced I was going to die on one of these swims. She didn't really care either way if I made it; she just wanted to know that I was OK. She said, 'Let this be the last, now.'

I laughed and said, 'I have seven swims to complete, Mum – I have four more to go.'

My dad's reaction, as always, was very excited for me as I had completed yet another one.

Although I was in a lot of pain, I was so happy. I'm sure the pain would have felt a lot worse if I hadn't made it – well, that's what I told myself. After a while I stepped out of the shower and as soon as I did my stomach started to burn again, without the warm water to soothe it. I tried ice and vinegar but nothing relieved it, so I had no choice but to go back and have another shower. All night I did this, back and forth; I must have had six or seven showers. I was desperate to sleep or at least just sit still, but due to the pain it became impossible to do so. In the early hours of the night, I wrapped up a towel full of ice and lay it on my stomach, which eased the pain slightly and I slept for about an hour and a half.

In the morning, reception told me the TV news had come to the hotel at around 9 a.m. but had been sent away so that I could rest; they had been told to come back at midday. I was very grateful for this, to have time to get some breakfast and not focus on anything for a while. At midday I was interviewed by KITV news reporter Andrew Pereira at the hotel, and then I relaxed for the rest of the day.

The station wanted me to come into the studio the following morning for a live interview, after which my crew and I headed out to the Pearl Harbor Visitor Center and the battleship USS *Missouri*. I still had my Equus Hotel T-shirt on from the morning show and a young girl passed me on the way to the entrance and congratulated me. She must have recognised me from the TV interview that morning. Our guide on the battleship tour looked at my shirt and said, 'I've seen a shirt like that before. A mad guy – think he was Australian – swam the Molokai Strait. Can you believe it he swam this!' he exclaimed, pointing out to the ocean.

'That was me,' I said.

'That was you? Wow! Didn't you get stung? Can I see it?'

I showed him the sting and he was beside himself with excitement and told the other tourists. The tour itself involved climbing up and down steps on the boat and was wasted on me. I visited each room and just sat down like a zombie in a chair. I wasn't in the mood for tourist trips, but it was nice for the others to see it. We stayed there most of the afternoon and then made our way back to the hotel.

For the next few days it was really hard to eat due to the ulcers. I was hungry after burning over 19,000 calories but it hurt a lot to eat so I was reduced to sucking on ice cubes, though I did move on to ice cream after a day or so.

I still wasn't 100 per cent clear on whether it had been a Portuguese man o' war or a box jellyfish that stung me. I looked on the internet and the stings seem to replicate those of a man o' war. When I later checked with a jellyfish specialist in Hawaii, she believed it was a man o' war rather than a box jellyfish. Both can kill you. A man o' war, which is actually made up of many organisms, has tentacles that can grow up to 100 feet in length. It feeds by paralysing its prey. It was clear I had been very lucky – the outcome could have been much worse. If you are stung by one you are supposed to go immediately to hospital. You shouldn't pull the tentacles off, which of course is what I had done in the water, not realising what was going on in the pitch-black. My stomach had swollen up significantly and it was as if I was fat on my left side, where the scars from the tentacles were highly visible.

On a positive note, by doing the swim just twenty-four hours after arriving, I at least now had twelve days left in Hawaii. The pressure was off and I could enjoy the rest of the trip. We travelled across the North Shore and explored the area. Honolulu is so beautiful, with its huge cliff faces, stunning beaches and friendly people. It is easy to see why so many people fall in love with the place.

When I was interviewed the next day by KITV about my next swim, I told them, 'Don't ask me about Catalina Channel now, as I'll say no chance.' I meant it at the time. Catalina Channel is 21 miles across, from an island in the Pacific to mainland Los Angeles. It was the next swim on my Ocean's Seven list and my plan was to do it the following year.

The plan didn't last long: when I was flying back from Hawaii I made the decision to try and swim it just a few months later. I didn't want to waste any unnecessary time and I had good fitness built up, so I thought, 'Why not?'

17

SWIM #4 CATALINA CHANNEL – TIME FOR A NIGHT SWIM

Catalina has a strict rule about booking sixty days in advance, so within a few weeks of arriving home I was booked in for the end of October. I knew it was a push for my shoulder to do two swims in one year, but having had a three-year gap due to the injury after the English Channel, I didn't want to waste any more time.

My wife and Chris weren't coming with me this time so I had to sort out a new crew. My friends Sue and Hugh, both open water swimmers, agreed to support me. Sue lives with her husband Con in LA and they offered to put me up, which was great. I managed to convince my boss to let me use what was left of my holiday and off I went on the plane again – only fourteen weeks after the last swim.

I felt confident, having successfully completed the toughest swim of my life in Hawaii, and I convinced myself this would be straightforward. The great thing about Catalina is that the weather is more often than not consistent, and you can normally go on your allocated day. This meant that I only had to book one week off work. The challenge is that you swim at midnight in complete darkness, so that you finish before the wind gets up in the afternoon. Like the Molokai Strait, Catalina is in the Pacific Ocean, but alongside the potential marine-life dangers I had experienced there, it has its own challenges – swimming it in the dark adds additional risks again.

I had three days before I was due to swim to acclimatise and get used to the time zone. Sue had very kindly checked out Catalina Island the week before so we knew where we were going. Each day I would train a little in the harbour, doing forty-five minutes to an hour, staying loose and keeping my head on the task in hand. I was very fortunate as Sue's house in LA was two minutes from the ocean, so I was spoilt and had easy access for training.

It was a little different from back in the UK, where I would have to travel three and a half hours to Dover or Windermere to get six hours' open-water training. I did train on and off at Colwick Park, Nottingham, which is a kilometre-long lake, but it was always a challenge if the ranger spotted me in there – he would usually ask me to leave because the fisherman complained. One time I was training there with Chris and after two hours we were told to get out. We managed to convince the ranger that we would swim at our own risk, that we were very experienced open-water swimmers, and that the risk to us both was very limited due to the fact that we had done several six-hour swims. Two hours later another ranger took over from the previous guy's shift and also tried to throw us out, but I managed to convince him to let us carry on by assuring him it would be my last ever six-hour swim in the lake. Shortly afterwards they set up an organised club and people can now swim for a couple of hours a few times a week.

The big day for my Catalina Channel swim came on 16 October 2012. Sue, Hugh and I had to get a ferry across to the island and the plan was to check into a hotel and relax before the swim. On the ferry ride across, Sue started speaking to a man about what I was doing. He was very interested and knew the strait very well. He understood where the swim would be leaving from, but pointed out that the ferry we were on didn't go there. It seemed we were in fact on the wrong ferry and heading to the wrong place! The location Sue had checked out the previous week wasn't the right part of the island after all. It was actually quite funny, although we did start to panic a little, worrying about how to get across to the right part as the swim was taking place in nine hours' time. Sue felt really bad about it, but it was just one of those things.

We looked at our options: hiring a car or getting another ferry. The ferry was a definite no as there were none going for the rest of the day, so we would have to try to get a car. The trouble was, we didn't know who to phone. Fortunately for us, some other people overheard the conversation and one lady said she would be driving that way and could drop us off. It was a huge relief. We had a further issue in that the truck was only big enough to fit two of us inside, but Hugh agreed to ride in the open back so it was all fine in the end.

The journey was a funny one and it helped me to relax, not thinking too much about the swim. The family were really nice, talking about the area, and they acted as tour guides. We took a real scenic route that was only open to locals with a specific permit.

After two hours we arrived at the hotel we had originally booked. By this time it was around 6.30 p.m. and so we walked to the nearest restaurant and had dinner. It felt like the Last Supper for me, but although there were some nerves I was as relaxed as I've been on any of the swims. I managed to get about two and a half hours' sleep back in the hotel room. Sue and Hugh were both happy to sleep on a sofa in the hotel lounge as they didn't want to disturb me.

I woke up around 10.30 p.m. and packed my things. It was only a five-minute walk to the harbour where the boat would pick us up and take us out to the starting point. Our meeting time was 11 p.m. and we would look to start around midnight. Just after 11 we could see the boat arriving in the distance – it was very eerie, like pirates coming out of the mist. It was so quiet and very dark.

The boat was huge – much bigger than any of the other boats on my previous three swims. I met the crew, who were really nice and made me feel at ease straight away. It took twenty-five minutes to get to the start and when we arrived I couldn't even see land.

I changed into my swim gear and Hugh greased my underarms and neck with Vaseline. I attached a couple of light sticks to my hat and swim trunks and as I slipped in I had to be pointed in the right direction. I may as well have closed my eyes, it was that dark. As I started swimming to shore, I was still struggling to make out where I needed to exit the water in accordance with the rules. After around 20 metres I started to make out where the land was and where to clear it. I reached the shore, shouted 'OK', and off I went.

It was still very eerie – I could hardly see my hand going into the water and it was hard not to wonder if something was underneath me or heading in my direction, as I wouldn't have been able to see it. These thoughts didn't last long, however; I reminded myself that, despite what I had gone through in the Molokai Strait, I had still been really confident that I would make it. I was certain that this swim couldn't possibly be as bad as that. I saw the dark as just another mental challenge to embrace – and I had experienced it before, so it wasn't going into the unknown. I had so far answered all the questions the ocean had to throw at me. This was just another swim.

As I swam, I kept seeing dark shadows. It was probably my mind playing tricks on me, or it could have been seaweed, which I swam into a couple of times and instantly thought it was a jellyfish. Although I couldn't see my hands, once they were in the water there was a strange type of luminosity that at the time seemed to make no sense in the darkness. I have since found out that this was down to a natural phenomenon called bioluminescence. This is the production and emission of light by a living organism, which occurs in marine vertebrates and invertebrates as well as in some fungi and microorganisms.

I initially started breathing to the left, towards the kayak and the boat. I felt uneasy doing this as I've always preferred breathing to the right, and so I asked after a little while if the kayak would move to the right of me so that I was in the middle. The kayaker, also called Adam, had green light sticks attached to the kayak and his head so I could clearly see him. The glare was quite strong and it took a while for my eyes to adapt to it. After forty-five minutes I started to feel sick; perhaps I was a little disorientated. I then swallowed some water and immediately started retching. As soon as this happens it always seems to trigger vomiting shortly afterwards.

I fed at the first hour on my usual carbohydrate powder, but I threw it up so it provided no benefit. I carried on and had another drink at two hours, again to the same effect. I asked my team for flat Coke on the next feed, which would be on the half hour from now on. I was really frustrated as I had to keep stopping and starting so early into the swim, and tensing up physically always makes me tense up mentally. I had been here so many times, which perhaps was part of the problem: I was almost expecting to be sick and my subconscious had associated ocean-swimming with sickness. I was anxious not to show any sign of distress as the observer and crew had gone extensively through safety regulations before the swim and I felt they wouldn't hesitate to get me out if they thought I was in trouble. I had been impressed with their thoroughness, although I didn't want it at the expense of my swim.

Just before my third feed I was sick again and I shouted out, 'Don't worry – this is normal and a good weight-loss programme!' in order to make light of the situation. From then on I made sure my team only gave me flat Coke. This seemed to do the trick: I stopped being sick and could get into a rhythm. Occasionally they would put a scoop of carbohydrate powder into the flat Coke without telling me, but it didn't affect me. The problem with the flat Coke was that, due to the caffeine, I would get a twenty-five-minute burst and then feel very low and weak, which is why it isn't a good idea to use it on a long-distance swim. But it always settled my stomach so I felt it was the best option at the time.

As I reached the four-hour mark, I was expecting to feel physically flat as I had in previous swims. On this occasion, however, I felt OK, but it hit me more as I reached five hours.

I was told sunrise would be at around 6 a.m. so I used that as an incentive, telling myself, 'Only one more hour before daylight, Adam – just get through this next hour.'

Sure enough light started to appear at 6 a.m., although the visibility was poor due to fog and I couldn't see more than about 20 yards in front of me. I also heard a screeching sound coming from the boat, which sounded a bit like a cat in distress. I looked over and the pilot was playing the bagpipes! I had heard he did this at sunrise, but it had slipped my mind – and if I'm honest it wasn't the greatest rendition of 'Danny Boy' in the world, so it came as a bit of a shock. It did, however, break the monotonous cycle so I was grateful for his not-so-sweet sound.

By now my left shoulder was really sore and I was struggling to pull properly with it. Something was badly wrong. It was serving little purpose and I was just allowing it to go through the motions and enter as comfortably as possible. I knew I had to switch off the pain and spend the remainder of the swim utilising the right arm to move forwards.

I was told around the five-hour mark that I had gone halfway, so in my mind it was all downhill from here; I started visualising the earth tilting and pushing me forward. The fog still wouldn't let up though, and I kept looking at the sky, hoping the sun would break out and give me some nice warmth on my back. Sadly for me, it didn't look like it would be doing that any time soon. I again reminded myself what I had been through in Hawaii; a shoulder packing in was a tiny obstacle in comparison. Prior to the swim I had convinced myself that this would be straightforward and I never doubted I would make it, but it was becoming much more difficult than I had anticipated. My speed had really slowed down due to the loss of power in my left arm, and as the hours passed by I couldn't see any sign of land.

Around the nine-hour mark, the fire service boat appeared and turned around to guide me in. The guys on board started shouting, 'Not far now – keep going, keep going!' It was a real positive boost for me and drove me on.

Apart from a couple of interested seals, I hadn't seen too much marine activity, but I knew that where there are seals there could potentially be sharks. When I experienced a sudden drop in temperature, it was a real shock to the system and I felt an instant shiver. I remembered hearing that three miles from shore the temperature can drop 2–3 degrees as you get closer to the mainland, so I knew land must be approaching. It had dropped to around 17 degrees, which is warmer than the English Channel, but when your body has become used to 19 degrees over a number of hours, those few degrees can make a big difference.

The pain in my left shoulder continued to intensify and required a considerable effort on every rotation. It was a real shame as I had been going so well with my new stroke for half of the swim; now it was just about staying in there and just getting the job done.

I tried to block out the pain as I had in Hawaii and kept repeating to myself again and again, 'Adam, this isn't as bad as a man o' war sting – just keep swimming!' I dreaded every left arm stroke and that side continued to serve no real purpose in terms of power. This concerned me; I knew if I compensated too hard with the right arm, there was a chance that the other shoulder could pack in as well. I couldn't afford to overdo it. The fog was still thick and there was no sign of land, which frustrated me, but I thought again about what Freda had said before the English Channel swim: never look at France. If you do, you will never take your eyes off it. It will appear to look closer than it is and therefore have a negative effect.

In this case, not seeing land frustrated me more as I had no idea if I was making any real progress. The fire service crew kept shouting to me, 'You're getting close!' The reality at this point was that I still had two and a half hours to go. I was leaning more on my bad shoulder and the speed was considerably slower than my normal pace. I was aware of approaching twelve hours as I had counted twenty-two feeds, and when we ignored the twelve-hour feed I knew I must be close. But there was still no sign of land. I had crossed halfway at the five-hour mark, but with the combination of my shoulder and currents the second half was taking much longer.

Finally, another ten minutes later, I saw land – and it looked less than 200 metres away. I wasn't sure whether I could trust my eyes and believe it was real, as I had gone so long without seeing anything. It was such a relief to see the finish line. I had grimaced my way through every stroke for the last six hours due to the pain, and as a result the swim had been much more difficult than I had envisaged. However, I knew now I was going to make it, and that is all that mattered at this moment.

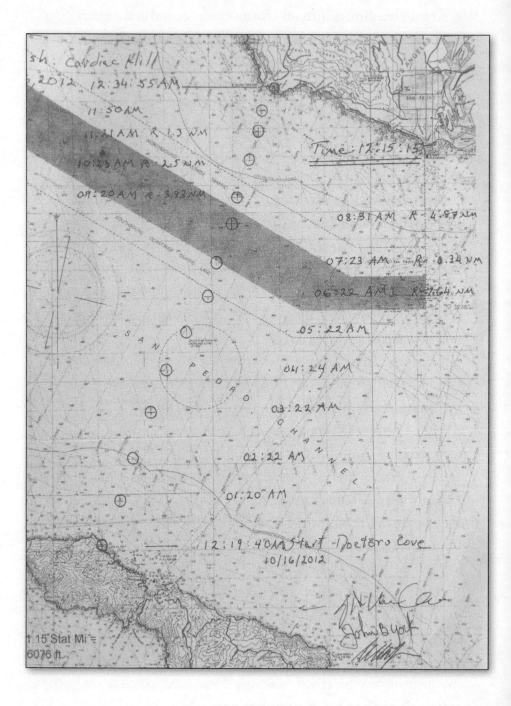

sh: *Cardiac Kill*
2012 12:34:55AM
11:50AM
11:21AM R-1.3 NM
10:23AM R-2.5 NM
09:20AM R-3.93 NM
Time: 12:15:15
08:31 AM R-4.87 NM
07:23 AM Rn 6.34 NM
06:22 AM R-7.64 NM
05:22 AM
04:24 AM
03:22 AM
02:22 AM
01:20 AM
12:19:40AM Start Doctor's Cove
10/16/2012

1.15 Stat Mi =
6076 ft.

At twelve hours fifteen minutes, I scrambled to my feet and clambered out of the water onto a rocky area. Standing on the rocks was a man I didn't know; he took pictures of me coming out. I thought it could have been a tourist, although it did seem strange that a tourist would choose to walk in this isolated spot. It turned out to be Forrest Nelson, another open-water swimmer. I was pleased to see a smiling face.

I was relieved to have completed another swim, but I knew it could be a while before the next one as something had gone in my shoulder. For now, though, I thought I would just enjoy the moment. I thanked my team and the crew and we made our way back to the harbour – mission accomplished!

I had a few more days left in LA before travelling back home, I felt so sore – not just in my shoulder but all over. I booked myself a massage and recuperated as much as I could. I went to watch a basketball game and saw a few tourist sites, including the Hollywood sign.

I had considered having a tattoo prior to travelling to LA, as I wanted something to remind me forever of the Ocean's Seven. I had watched a reality show on TV called *LA Ink*, about a tattoo studio in which some of the best tattooists in the world worked, and I thought if I ever had one done it would have to be there. I loved the idea, inspired by a television advert, of white horses coming out of the waves, to signify determination. I visited the shop and explained to the artist what I wanted. He said if I wanted lots of horses he would have to tattoo my whole back. I definitely wasn't that brave, so it would have to be just one horse, which I wanted inside my arm on my biceps. I was more nervous about having the tattoo done than I was about doing any of the swims. I made the decision to go for it; for me it represents motivation and the will to succeed. Two years later my tattoo became the logo for my business, Ocean Walker.

18

WHEN ONE DOOR CLOSES, ANOTHER ONE OPENS

Going back to work was again really tough. I knew my holiday allowance had been used up and it would be a while before the next swim.

But I didn't waste any time getting an appointment with my surgeon. I knew the shoulder was bad – it was the same familiar dull ache I had previously experienced. I was worried as I didn't have private healthcare now, and I knew no insurer would cover my troubled shoulder even if I did invest. I had never let money get in the way of my swims, but I knew I was up against it if I had to pay thousands of pounds for the next swim as well as my surgery. The surgeon said, if I went privately, he'd be able to operate at the end of December or in January. It was the end of October now and I had already provisionally booked Tsugaru Strait for August of the following year. Even if I had the surgery straight away I knew it was going to be a big ask to rehabilitate and allow myself enough time to get back to full fitness. I asked how long it would be if I waited to have it done for free on the National Health Service. He estimated it could be up to a year. I didn't want to lose yet another year to injury, and told him I would think about it.

For a couple of weeks I debated what to do. I knew my parents would help me with the costs if I really wanted to go privately, but I would have felt bad as they had done so much already to support me on my swims and the operation could be a lot of money. Eventually the decision was made for me: I received a phone call from the surgeon's secretary to say an appointment had become available in January on the NHS, so it wouldn't cost me anything. I was so happy. I thought there might still be a chance to do the swim in August after all.

It was a very difficult time in my personal life as well. My wife and I had drifted apart and made the decision to separate. When she decided not to come and support me on my Catalina swim, I knew deep down it was over. Although it was the right decision, there was a lot to sort out. In addition I didn't know whether to train as I would be having surgery in a few months' time. My job wasn't secure and so there was a question mark over the stability of my working life, on top of the mental strain of a separation and everything that comes with that.

I kept dragging myself to train, but I found it difficult staying focused. My brain was saying, 'What's the point? Your shoulder is knackered and your life is a mess.' It took everything I had to not stop training and feel sorry for myself instead. My mind was scrambled with negativity and I couldn't see a way forward. I knew I had to keep training – it was the only thing that seemed to make sense in my life at this time.

I can't explain why the swims meant so much and why I had to complete them; there was just something in my head telling me to continue now more than ever.

I moved in with my parents and felt that I had hit rock-bottom. I was also really scared about what the surgeon would find – I knew the last operation hadn't been a complete success. What if I had caused irreparable damage after another four big swims? I made a decision: whatever the result of the operation, even if I had to swim with just one arm for the remaining three swims, it wouldn't prevent me from achieving my dream.

As the date for the operation grew closer, I knew I had to break the cycle and not allow myself to be so down with the shoulder problems and other issues in my life. On this particular morning, I was travelling to London for a meeting at my company's showroom. I caught the train at Newark North Gate, which is only an hour and a half to King's Cross. The second stop was Peterborough and as we approached they announced that the train had broken down and we all had to get off and wait for another. The train was really busy and so the platform was full of people. I happened to look up and there was a girl who really stood out – she had some fancy tights on and caught my eye. I went to get a hot drink and contemplated making conversation, which was strange as it would have been completely out of character. I mean, what would I say? 'Hi! How are you? It's a shame the train broke down.' Not exactly the best chat-up line in the world. I then thought she looked cold, so I'd just say, 'You look cold', and figure out where to go from there. It didn't seem a great plan, but what did I have to lose? I started walking towards her but when I was inches away and about to speak, a voice behind me said, 'Hi, Adam – how are you doing?' It was a colleague of mine, going to the same place as I was. I turned around and walked in the opposite direction towards her. My chance had gone. But it had been a silly plan, I told myself, and she had probably saved me from a huge embarrassment.

The new train arrived and I carried on with my day. On the way back in the afternoon, however, I saw her again and sat in front of her on the train. The seats were far too tall to peer over and there was no way I could just start chatting. As I was trying to devise another plan, I looked up and saw, almost in slow motion, a suitcase making its way off a shelf and landing on a passenger's head, cutting it open. I quickly rushed to the toilet to get some tissue to help him, and fortunately he was OK. I turned around to the girl behind me and said, 'Did you see that?'

'No, what?' she asked.

Her name was Gemma. She had missed the whole incident but I was now talking to her. I'm sure there must have been an easier way to get chatting, but I was grateful to the man and to the case that fell on his head!

We talked and exchanged details, and then started seeing each other. It was nice to meet a like-minded person who wanted the same things as I did.

I advised work about the upcoming operation and the fact that I wouldn't be able to drive into work for a few weeks. Fortunately for me, my boss was also a friend; he was very lenient, considering how much time I had taken off. Most bosses would probably have fired me by now – it was very apparent that the swimming was more of a priority to me than the job.

The operation was scheduled for 22 January. I was pleased

when it came around because I wanted to begin my training for Japan. I was more nervous this time as it was my third operation and I knew there could potentially be a lot of damage.

I was asked how strong I wanted the anaesthetic and I said I would take the minimum amount as I wanted to hear what the surgeon said. I wish I hadn't – I could hear him say things like 'diseased tissue' and 'Oh, no – it's detached again!' I was scared to look at the monitor as I didn't want to know that the shoulder was too bad to continue chasing my goal. I knew it would crush me. At one point I went into shock and they increased the anaesthetic. When I woke up, my blood pressure was very low and I was shivering. My core temperature was under 35 degrees, so mildly hypothermic.

After the operation, the surgeon told me that the tendon had detached itself and was, in his words, 'of no use'; they had to cut it. This meant that there would always be a weakness there and I would never have the same strength as in my right arm. There was no time to dwell on it, though: I had to focus on getting fit again and time was ticking before the next swim. I purposely didn't mention the swims to the surgeon; I didn't want to be put off.

My arm was immobilised in a sling for six weeks and it wasn't until the end of May that I could do some light swimming. By June I felt I was able to start training properly again, which gave me ten weeks of swimming before Japan. To say it was a tough task to get to the level of fitness required for the Tsugaru Strait is an understatement. The only positive thing for me was that the swim was 15 miles, shorter than any of the previous swims, although the tides there are some of the strongest in the world. I convinced myself that I was due for some luck and I hoped the ocean gods would be kind.

I worked hard to become as fit as possible in that short time as my shoulder remained sore after the operation. I was even more delicate with my hand entry on my stroke and just used my pulling arm to guide it forward. This increased my efficiency and saved more energy – I seemed to glide even more than I did previously. I knew I wasn't as fit as I had been for Molokai or Catalina as I couldn't hold my times for as long. But my desire to make it was as big as ever and I approached this swim with a positive mindset. I had to keep telling myself I was in control of my own destiny.

My head was filled with other pressures: I still had to generate the funds and the job was still in the balance. In addition I was trying to sell my old house and deal with separation issues. I couldn't do anything about the house and job but I was determined not to let money get in the way of my dreams. We put on a fundraiser for the swim and to support Whale and Dolphin Conservation. Gemma's rock band, Reckless, helped out by providing the live entertainment. Gemma has sung from a young age; she is one of those people who oozes talent and she can sing pretty much anything, while being extremely modest with it. I also had raffle and auction prizes from a number of generous friends including my physiotherapist Tracy Gjertson and sports remedial masseuse Dean Haspey. (I owe these guys a lot as they also worked tirelessly with me, ensuring I was in the best possible physical shape in order to take on the remaining swims.) The cost was over £8,000 so I knew I had no option – I had to succeed as there would be no chance of doing it again.

This was the first time Gemma would see me in a channel swim. We discussed what is involved with the feeds and what to look out for. She asked me, 'How would I know when the right time would be to get you out if you are in trouble?' I told her there was no right time and I wouldn't be getting out until the finish, so she didn't need to worry. I had never thought about this before and hadn't been asked, and I didn't want to give myself a choice. As far as I was concerned, the boat wasn't there and I simply had to swim across. It is always sensible to have a contingency plan on a channel swim, but you won't get a swimmer wanting to discuss or think about it. Therefore you will need to prepare to do your own tests if necessary, asking them questions and monitoring their stroke rate – if it reduces significantly it can be a sign of hypothermia.

It is good to have at least two people on the boat – if one gets seasick you will at least have another person there to give you drinks and food, as well as looking out for any issues and generally supporting you. It was a great mental boost knowing that John Raynor, a childhood friend, would be coming along on the boat to support me. He now lived in Japan and it would be a six-hour drive for him.

19

SWIM #5 TSUGARU STRAIT – AGAINST ALL ODDS

The flight to Tokyo was a long one – twelve hours in total – and we then had to get a train north for three and a half hours, only to be picked up by John and driven a further hour and a half to Aomori, which was near the starting point of the swim. We arrived and caught a very overcrowded train – Gemma and I sat on the floor in the doorway for most of the journey (not the ideal preparation for a long swim), but for the last forty minutes I managed to convince the train conductor to let us sit in first class as we were exhausted. I think he felt sorry for us. What I love about the Japanese people is how polite they are. I blocked the doorway for hours and every time the train conductor came past he had to step over me but still he bowed out of respect. I can't ever imagine that happening in the UK. In London they would have told me to shift, in no uncertain terms, or maybe even trampled over me.

By the time we arrived it was evening, and although I offered to put John up in a hotel, he was happy to camp and I helped him to pitch his tent. There was nothing else there apart from a hotel situated on the top of a cliff overlooking the sea, and a campsite; the nearest shop was an hour and a half away. It was very remote and very beautiful. We checked into the hotel and I couldn't help but laugh: the Japanese tend to be small in stature and the shower had an extremely low ceiling with about enough room to wash my feet. I am 6 foot 5 inches in height, so it didn't really work for me. I didn't care, though; it was a great place to rest up and try to relax for the next few days.

I realised I hadn't taken the correct charger for the shark defence unit. I tried to charge it with one designed for a different appliance, but the following morning the red light on the side of the unit was still flashing showing it hadn't fully charged. This was an irritation that I really didn't need! My options were really limited as my swim was scheduled for sometime in the next two or three days and the supplier would struggle to send one out to me by then. I didn't know what to do – it was the Pacific Ocean and I'd already had a number of shark sightings in previous swims. I spoke to John and he agreed we should drive to the nearest electrical shop, over an hour away, and see if we could get anything to fit the unit. It was a complete long shot, but I thought it was worth a go. Fortunately for me, John is fluent in Japanese – they didn't seem to speak much English in these parts. We arrived at the electrical shop and John explained our predicament. I could read the confusion on the salesman's face. I guess it's not every day he gets asked if he has a charger to fit an electrical shark defence unit. He explained to John that the charger for an electronic massage chair would fit. The issue was that the chair cost $8,000 and there was no guarantee the charger would work. I weighed up the options of taking a massage chair home with me in excess baggage in order to potentially protect me from sharks. I decided that maybe this wasn't a good idea – I would just take my chances.

We drove back to the hotel and on route I managed to get hold of Mika, who would be my observer on the boat and the English-speaking translator for the pilot. We agreed to meet with Mika and the pilot, Captain Mizushima, at 3 p.m. to discuss the swim. Mika explained that the start of the swim would be from a rock, which would take us an hour and a half to get to by boat. She also explained the very strong complex currents and the importance of speed if the current changes. Realistically, if the current is too strong, the pilot might have to make the decision to end the swim; I would have to follow the pilot's instructions. Captain Mizushima was a very small chap, less than 5 feet tall. I looked like a giant next to him and he didn't speak a word of English, just smiled a lot.

The swim was going to be between Honshu and Hokkaido, island to island. I knew that no individual had crossed the channel this year and I sensed the magnitude of the swim. I just hoped the currents would be kind. I asked Mika to tell the pilot that I had done big swims before and that he didn't need to be concerned about my capability. I am always conscious that a pilot can take a swim out of the swimmer's hands if the conditions become unfavourable, and I wanted him to know that I had gone through some tough swims previously.

I asked how many days it would be before we could potentially go and the reply I got was 'Tonight'. It was Molokai all over again – no rest, no time for acclimatisation, just straight into it. I thought it was good to have come just before my scheduled swim date, as I had 2 weeks holiday I could take off work, and I knew this strait was unpredictable. If the weather conditions weren't favourable to begin with, it would at least give me the opportunity to wait until it settled. Not that it always works out that way, but I thought better safe than sorry. I had waited nine days before swimming Gibraltar and finally went on the last possible day before returning home.

The plan was to meet up again at 2 a.m., just over nine hours later, so I knew time was against me. We said our goodbyes and went back to the hotel to start organising things. I had an early dinner in the hotel restaurant with the most unbelievable view of the Tsugaru Strait. The hotel was on top of a cliff and you could see across the strait. For most people this would be a good thing, but for me, being reminded of what I was going to take on in a few hours' time made me feel sick to my stomach. They had big glass windows in the restaurant and lounge areas, and you couldn't help but look out. All the stresses and strains of my job, selling my house, my divorce, my lack of training, lack of time to acclimatise to the conditions or time zone, and lack of operational shark unit, started to manifest themselves in my brain. I sat there eating fish and looking out at this vast ocean, with no clue where I was going to start or end as I couldn't see any land. It really affected me and I felt quite emotional. I wanted to achieve this so badly. My life felt upside down but the swimming was a constant. These were more than just swims to me – they were a huge part of who I was now.

I said to Gemma, 'I have to get across. There is no other option!' She hadn't seen me like this before. The ocean has a way of making you feel vulnerable, no matter how tough you think you are.

I tried to explain to the waiter what I was about to do and asked could I have some meat for energy, rather than just fish. I was feeling a little tired from the journey so needed something to pick me up. They were great, bringing out a big selection, and although I wasn't too hungry I forced myself to eat it.

We went back to the hotel room and began preparing the equipment and drinks, shaking up the Coke bottles to release the gas. As there was no kettle on this boat, John had provided us with several large thermos flasks. Gemma boiled the kettle in the room and filled the flasks up so that I could still have warm drinks out at sea. By this time it was 7.30 p.m. and I had seven hours to try and get some rest. I lay on the bed, put my headphones on and listened to my motivational CD. Clem's CDs had really helped me, since Molokai, to focus. I played them over and over again as I couldn't sleep. It could have been due to jet lag as well as nerves: Japan is eight hours ahead of the UK, so it was actually lunchtime back at home.

I was particularly anxious – more so than normal. I tried to keep my mind free of the devil on my shoulder, as I knew it would only take one negative thought about my lack of training to spiral into self-doubt. I've realised it can take a lot of focus to keep a clear mind, but if you get into the habit of not overthinking the swims it does get easier – but you have to continuously work at it.

I remembered getting a good night's sleep before both the English Channel and Gibraltar, but there was more going on in my head now and I resorted to walking around the room, still listening to my motivational CD. I think I eventually fell asleep around 11.30 p.m., so I at least managed to get a couple of hours rest.

At 1.30 a.m. the alarm went off and it was time to wake up. John met us in reception just before 2 a.m. and we made our way to the bottom of the hill to meet up with the pilot. It was really windy so I was worried the sea would be choppy and we wouldn't be able to go. We lifted everything on board and off we went to the harbour to assess the conditions. The time now was 2.30 a.m. and it was going to take about an hour and a half to get to the starting point in Honshu.

John, having no experience of supporting a swimmer on a channel swim, had brought a deckchair, which did make me laugh. I thought, 'He's got no chance if he thinks he's going to sun himself!' John sat on his chair in the middle of the fishing boat and I wedged myself at the back, where I could see the horizon in case I felt sick, as I often do when it's choppy. It worked out to be a good decision as the boat was swinging all over the place, with the rain coming in sideways. Poor John looked green and halfway into the journey was sick over the side. I felt sorry for him – there is nothing worse than being sick on a boat and having no option but to put up with it. And we hadn't even started the swim yet! Gemma was fine – she was enjoying the boat ride, having never experienced anything like it before.

Mika came over to speak to us and said they were taking their time getting us to the start due to the weather conditions; if this continued, there was no way we could go ahead with the swim. I continued to play my hypnotherapy CD and among the crashing of the waves and the rain coming in sideways I could hear Clem's calming voice in my ears saying, 'Just relax.' It made me chuckle as I could see at the same time John being sick and the boat rocking all over the place.

At this point I convinced myself I wasn't going. I said to

Gemma, 'There is no way we can go out in this – it's far too rough.' I had never talked negatively like this before – it wasn't like me. But I thought I'd been given a lifeline having had next to no sleep, and everything felt wrong to go. I told her, 'I'd prefer to go tomorrow and get some rest.'

Gemma said, 'OK, but you need to make sure, if we do, that you don't leave the hotel room but just sleep.'

I agreed and, as my decision was made, I felt relaxed and even began to joke a little. Another hour later we arrived 15 metres from the rocks in Honshu, which was the starting point of the swim. Mika said we would wait a while to see if the weather improved. It was very rough and I was convinced we wouldn't go. In the previous swims I was ready to go whatever the weather, so it was a concern that I was thinking this way. I went to the toilet at the back of the boat, which was so small I couldn't shut the door. It made me laugh, sitting on the toilet rocking back and forth, looking out at the ocean. I thought, 'There are worse views whilst sitting on the toilet, I guess!'

After around thirty minutes of waiting, the pilot appeared with a beaming smile. Mika translated his words: he believed the weather would improve as we got closer to the Hokkaido side. I asked what the weather would be like tomorrow and the thought was much of the same – could be better and could be worse. The trouble with this sport is that you can't predict the conditions; if it was worse tomorrow I might miss my chance, as I now only had a two-day window. Mika then asked me, 'Are you prepared to swim in this?'

I didn't know what to do. I thought for a few seconds and went with my instinct: 'OK, let's do it.' I felt like saying 'no' but going the next day would somehow be giving in to the channel and showing weakness.

I put on my swim hat and goggles. Gemma helped do the greasing under the arms and back of the neck with Vaseline and I slid off the side of the boat heading in the direction of the start point. I swam very slowly to the rocks, trying to save energy before I started the actual swim. This was a very different approach from when I swam the English Channel solo. On reflection it was a bad move: I was obviously concerned that my energy levels were low, so I was starting with the wrong mindset.

I fiddled with my goggles, delaying further, and then put my arms in the air to say I was ready, and off I went. In previous swims I had set off like a rocket, but this start was much more subdued. Perhaps I was subconsciously thinking I would need all my energy and so didn't want to go off too quickly. This wasn't my normal confident mentality before a swim.

I was definitely anxious and couldn't even decide which side of the boat to swim on. I went to my favoured left side, then convinced myself I would be faster and use less energy swimming on the right and breathing left, so I switched. In training I am slightly faster breathing left as I pull harder with the right arm just after breathing due to the biceps tendon issue in my left shoulder.

After just thirty minutes I took a gulp of water and started to be sick. As I've mentioned previously, I am no stranger to being sick, but it does disrupt my rhythm and my relaxed state of swimming. I had unfortunately become used to this irritation and I just saw it as one of the many mental tests open-water swimming puts me through. I always convince myself it will finish at some point. But I had never been so sick so early into a swim, and with everything else that had happened up to this point, it was the last thing I needed. I hadn't got off to a good start and the devil was well and truly trying to get in my head, telling me it was over when it had hardly begun. I turned my thoughts back to where they needed to be, like on previous swims: 'It's just one arm in front of the other . . . Forget everything else.' It was evident my mind was not in the right place, but I remembered what had happened in Hawaii, my shoulder operation and how much I needed this – even more so after all the disruption in my life.

I switched back to the left side of the boat to stick with what I was comfortable with. I was sick on and off for the first four hours, trying to not let it affect my thoughts and just get to the next feed.

At the four-hour mark, I was waved over to the boat by Mika and she said the strong current was pushing us eastward, so I had to swim faster or we would be pushed off course. I asked how long for and she replied, 'Until we tell you to stop!'

Not the answer I was looking for. I asked if I could have an estimate. Mika spoke to the pilot and replied, 'Maybe thirty minutes.'

I had no choice now but to concentrate on speed. In some ways it was a good thing as I had no time to think about sickness or my personal and work issues. I had been warned by the pilot that the currents could change at any time and I had also read that it can be impossible to cross if they are too strong. I tried not to think about it. My only thought was to get past this first hurdle by beating the current.

I swam as fast as I could, trying not to overthink it and to keep as calm as possible. I went close to my full pace and kept an eye on the crew, waiting for some reaction or signal that I could slow down. I pushed hard for around twenty minutes and then saw Mika and my crew signalling to me that I could ease off. I fell back into my normal pace. I had kept on course for now, but I wondered when the next moment would come to do it again. I tried to convince myself it had been a one-off.

It was wishful thinking. After a short period of twenty minutes or so, I saw the pilot look at his monitor and call Mika over. They told me I had to push again. I went up the gears and started swimming like my life depended on it; after twenty-five minutes or so I could ease off again. I remained calm, but it was now in my mind that I might have to do this all the way across, and I was clinging to the hope that this wouldn't be the case.

I had never faced this kind of brutal challenge before. I had had my battles with currents and tide, but not this pressure to swim so fast this early on. The sickness had stopped, which was just as well as there was no time to stop for that. The next few hours consisted of sprints, limited rest and then sprinting again. There was only one occasion, around the six-hour mark, when I was told to sprint because the current was in my favour. It didn't last long, though, and before long it was slow going again. At the start I tried to make it into a joke, saying to Mika, 'Let me guess: I have to sprint again.' After a while, however, the joke had worn thin. Shortly afterwards John attempted to motivate me by saying, 'Good news – you're almost half way!' This only served to upset me more, at the thought of how long I had to go; however, he meant well by it.

The waves were not letting up either, and although the pilot believed the conditions would improve as we got closer to Hokkaido, the reality was quite the opposite. Around nine hours in, it was like I was swimming uphill.

John said, 'You've probably got ten minutes of this and it will improve.'

Sadly he too was mistaken: it went on for a good hour and then calmed down slightly, but it was still very choppy. I came in for a feed and everyone looked a bit glum. I thought everyone would expect me to be down so I'd do the opposite and make a joke of it.

'If anyone has anything positive to say,' I told them, 'now's the time!' No response from Gemma or John, so I said, 'No? No. OK, I'll carry on, then', in a sarcastic tone.

I then started swimming in front of the boat for a few seconds and I shouted to the pilot, 'Come on! I haven't got all day to wait for you!' He of course didn't understand a word of what I was saying and just smiled.

The pilot was a nice little fella. When Mika told me to sprint, he would occasionally punch the air to fire me up and have a beaming smile. On one feed, Mika told me, 'He's never seen some one with so much power – how you can just pick up the pace.' Hearing this gave me a real boost and was just what I needed to hear to push me on.

I'm not sure where the energy was coming from; I felt flat and finished after two hours and I had sprinted on and off for nearly eleven hours. I could only put it down to desire – I felt like I found more energy and speed than I ever had before. I was desperately trying to stay in with a chance of completing the swim. I knew if I eased off on any of those sprints I might not be able to get back on course and the swim would be over.

At eleven hours thirty minutes, the choppy seas were in full force – it was as if the sea was fighting against itself and I had no chance of developing any kind of rhythm. I decided to change sides of the boat. I felt having the boat on my left side would encourage me to swim in the right direction.

I couldn't believe I could see land – this was the first time I actually truly believed I was going to finish the swim. I thought I had done the hard work and I wasn't going to fail now!

Just as I thought that, the ocean gods unleashed more rough water on me, with swells 10–12 feet high. I had never been in such rough seas in the middle of a channel before. I was getting bounced around like a pinball. I couldn't believe it. I thought, 'What have I done to deserve this?' I was hardly making any headway at all.

John was nearest to me in my eyeline when I breathed and Gemma was up at the front of the boat. I couldn't see her full face, though I could sense she was upset as she had her head in her hands. As I breathed to John, through a slightly steamed-up goggle I could see him smiling away at me. I felt exhausted from all the sprinting I had done. My pace had been taken right back and I struggled at times to search for the most efficient spot to put each arm in the water as I was lifted up and down and pushed from side to side.

I started to get emotional – not from tiredness or pain, but from wanting to swim across so badly and watching it being taken away. I was left helpless in the face of the ocean's power and all I could do was stay with it and pray that the conditions would subside and I could carry on producing enough energy to keep going. My heart was pounding so hard that I thought it was going to burst through my chest. My breaths were getting shorter and shorter and it was hard to find where to get enough oxygen as the chop was so constant.

Gemma said, 'You should get this for another ten minutes or so and it will calm down.'

I didn't know whether this was true or whether she was simply wishing for that outcome. I have found in these swims, very much as in life, if you have hope it's easier to carry on with optimism.

I came in to the boat for a drink and was being thrown around like a ragdoll; I couldn't stay in one spot to drink and I watched the boat swing from one side to the other. I could barely speak. I turned to Gemma and said the worst thing you can ever say to a loved one in this particular situation: 'My heart is going so fast, I think I'm going to have a heart attack.'

As soon as I said it I thought what an insensitive thing it was to say. I just wanted to share how bad I was feeling. Maybe it was my brain trying to find an excuse in case the swim didn't go my way, or it was the devil on my shoulder slowly trying to break me. I had a little sip of the drink, but by now, like in the Molokai swim, I was beyond wanting to drink and take nutrition on board.

I carried on through the washing-machine waves, breathing to the boat and watching John continue to smile. I went through so many emotions, from feeling sad to pleading with the ocean to subside and calm down. The ocean wasn't listening: there was no sign of it calming down and the more it went on, the more frustrated I became. At one stage I fist-punched the water whilst in mid-stroke, which served no purpose apart from hurting my hand for a few seconds. I had to keep focused, conserve as much energy as possible and switch off mentally, as I had done so many times before. Frustration and anger were only wasting energy and serving no purpose or benefit.

After one and a half hours, I finally accepted the conditions and tried to look at the positives. I said to myself, 'Now, think about this, Adam: with every arm stroke you're getting closer. It may be slow going, but you are edging towards land.' It certainly was slow going: I apparently covered 800 metres in an hour through the worst waves and at other times I was averaging over 4 kilometres an hour.

Two hours later, the sun began to fall behind my destination, creating a silhouette of land, which helped me to see it more clearly. Finally the water began to settle, feeling calmer, and the tension in my body eased. I became more relaxed. It felt like I was on the final straight home. I convinced myself that I had gone through everything the ocean could throw at me for one day and finally it was time to do the last part and finish it. I had made this mistake before, thinking I was near completion and having to face the disappointment of carrying on. I was experienced in what could happen so it wouldn't be as much of a shock to the system this time, but I had burned through most of my energy and I prayed I had now done enough.

I asked how long to go and John said, 'Less than two miles.'

I had asked the same question an hour and a half earlier and it had been just over two miles, but somehow hearing that it was just less than this seemed so much better. We appeared to turn more with the current and the land was now in front of me instead of to the east. There wasn't much of a break following the killer chop that I had just swum through and the rolling waves that now hurled themselves towards me. I thought, 'At least I can breathe easier through this.' Each wave took approximately five seconds to come over the top of me. I tried to bodysurf as one after another rolled up and over.

After thirty minutes it was obvious that I didn't appear to be getting any closer. I thought, 'This two miles is taking a long time!' Another thirty minutes went by and I was starting to get concerned. It was becoming dark so I shouted to the boat in a frustrated voice, 'What is happening?'

John replied, 'The tide is pushing you back – just ease off until it turns.'

For as long as I had known John he had always been completely honest. I would have preferred a more positive response but at least I knew where I stood. I continued on, with the waves steamrolling over me. I now knew that gliding on the waves was of no benefit whatsoever; my only option was to get back into swimming normally. I couldn't believe it – I had thought the waves would just take me in. I was once again annoyed with the ocean, but I had to keep pushing on.

We had another safety boat throughout the swim which was consistently 100 yards ahead. Its main purpose was to avoid fishing nets, the reason being that these nets cost a lot of money, and for many people in this area, fishing is the main source of income. Having another vessel up ahead allowed the main safety boat next to me to focus on guiding me across. At this point we were still approximately two miles from finishing, so they made their way to my left side, around 15 metres away.

At that moment, for some reason, I thought about my electronic shark unit not working and happened to look down into the deep, wondering if there was anything down there. This was out of character for me, as I had become so used to switching off any negatives and not focusing on 'what lies beneath'. Just as I did that, I saw a large shadow swim underneath me. I was convinced it was a shark. I started shouting at the boat, 'Come closer – I've just seen a shark!' I had mentioned a previous shark sighting five hours into the swim and I reminded myself of Hawaii and that this was also the Pacific Ocean, with similar potential shark dangers.

The boat was swaying back and forth; no one looked safe on

there. I glanced over in between each swim stroke, watching them clutching the sides for fear of falling in. I started to think that maybe I was better off in the water! I sprinted to come up by the side of the boat, but it seemed to be getting further away. I now felt a little nervous and exposed, as the darkness had set in and I was still thinking about what I had seen. Eventually I managed to make it close enough.

'Did you not hear me shouting I had a shark swim near me?'

'We couldn't get near you,' Gemma said. 'The boat is swaying all over the place and it was too dangerous.'

A decision was made to put light sticks on the back of my goggles so that they could see me. I was handed a new pair of goggles with the lights attached. After a further minute or two, I felt something brush over my face. I thought I must have swum into a jellyfish or something. I then realised the goggles had some string attached and this was dangling over the top of my head onto my face. It was quite irritating, but I didn't have the energy to adjust it so I kept swimming with it brushing over my face and hampering my view. The upshot was that it distracted me from thinking about the shark.

I had been told an hour ago that the lighthouse was the finish and that's where we were aiming for. It now seemed so close, but in open water distance can be deceiving, as I knew all too well. When I swam the English Channel, France looked so close at one point when it was actually five hours away. The pilot had already said to John in Japanese that he was concerned about the suffering I had endured on the swim and how much more I could take. John thought it sounded as if he was considering pulling me out, so politely just walked away from the conversation so as not to debate it with him.

Another thirty minutes went by. I had another feed, but at this point I was taking very little fluid in so once again it didn't serve much purpose apart from allowing my crew to check on me and keep my spirits up.

The support crew are pivotal in a marathon swimmer's success – what they say and do can be the difference between completing a swim or not. They not only decide what food and drink to give you to keep your energy levels up, but they are also your eyes to watch for any marine life or obstacles that you want to avoid. In addition, they ensure you keep an efficient swimming line so you don't waste any unnecessary energy and are kept safe. They also act as your motivators when times get tough and they can react to any situation to support you. It takes a certain type of character to be effective as support crew; I recommend someone with a calm head, positive in nature and whom you fully trust to make the right decision when required – to pull you out, if necessary. Their role should not be underestimated.

I had now swum fifteen hours and gone through so many emotions, from believing it wasn't going to happen to being sure it was, and then convinced it wasn't again. I tried to stay calm. I knew we were close to finishing, although the last two and a half hours had shown that that meant nothing.

Another twenty minutes went by and I was getting really fed up now, cursing and shouting at the ocean in my mind: 'Haven't you done enough to me? You've proven how hard you are to cross. I will stay out here all week, if I have to, so you may as well let me in!' My relationship with the ocean had been challenged during the previous swims and I thought the Molokai Strait had thrown everything possible at me. But this was as bad as anything I had encountered previously; the conditions had been relentless and unforgiving.

After my rant, the pilot suddenly appeared at the edge of the boat and gave a flat hand signal. John and Gemma then shouted, 'No current!'

I shouted back, 'How long to go?'

John responded, 'Seven hundred metres.'

I was still suspicious – the ocean hadn't behaved itself today – but I wasn't going to hang around. I suddenly sprang into life, gritting my teeth, and I swam like my life depended on it, counting sixty strokes, then another sixty, then another sixty. I kept saying in my mind, 'Don't you dare change, current – don't you dare!'

Suddenly I could see the bright light off the rocks where the lighthouse was. It was just twenty metres away. I still didn't trust the current, so I continued to power on with everything I had. I saw rocks in front of me and wasn't sure whether I should climb on them as there was another cluster to the side of me. I went to the nearest one and quickly scampered out to clear the water for fear the current might change. I put my arms in the air, which was a task in itself as they felt so heavy and knowing I had done it had made my body go limp.

I could barely believe it. With such little training and after believing it was impossible to sprint at four hours after being so sick, I had managed to find a way when there appeared to be none.

I was so exhausted and sore that it was a struggle to swim back to the boat. Now the adrenaline was gone, swimming front crawl seemed impossible. I did a very gentle breaststroke back to the boat, as I had after the English Channel. I climbed aboard and gave Gemma and John a hug. This swim had

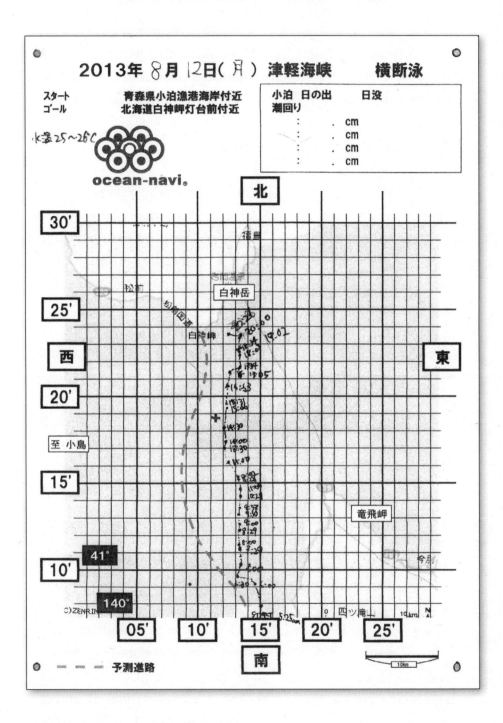

taken me to hell and back. It took me fifteen hours thirty-one minutes of constant battling, but I had managed to park the emotional baggage I had been carrying in my mind throughout this challenge and complete the swim against all the odds.

20

BOOIE – MY BEST FRIEND AND SWIMMING SOULMATE

I was now one step closer to my ultimate goal of completing the Ocean's Seven and the feeling of euphoria was once again something that couldn't be surpassed in my everyday life.

The journey back to base took just under three hours. We sat at the back of the boat looking up at the stars and just taking in everything that had just happened as the ocean sprayed our faces. Gemma caught sight of not one but two shooting stars, which she thought was some kind of sign. When we arrived back to the hotel, they had very kindly laid out a banquet in my room. I was really hungry and tried to eat a spoonful of rice, but soon realised my mouth was so swollen and sore with ulcers that it hurt to swallow. I had to leave it again.

I had a shower and went to bed. I managed to sleep until around 4 a.m. before I woke up and couldn't get back to sleep due to the soreness in my shoulders. The muscular pain

I was experiencing was actually a lot less than I had after previous long-distance swims. I could really feel the difference now that I was swimming more efficiently, but this swim had been so physically demanding, and had come so soon after an operation, that it had taken a lot out of me. I decided to have a walk in the lobby; I felt quite awake, which was probably a combination of adrenaline and jet lag, as I had only left the UK two days ago.

As I had swum early in the trip again, it meant we had ten days to explore Japan. That day I met up with Mika to thank her for all of her support. She had played a crucial role in communicating back to me the commands of the Japanese-speaking pilot, Captain Mizushima. The same day I also met a Guatemalan swimmer called Yesenia and her sister. Yesenia was attempting to swim the strait that evening. I asked her if she had all the energy drinks and equipment she needed.

She said 'I haven't got any drinks – I will go to the shop.'

I responded, 'There aren't any shops for miles. We are in the middle of nowhere. I have some, if you want it?'

As luck would have it, my drink was the same one she used in training. You should never try a drink or food for the first time on a channel swim – it's important you train with it first. I couldn't understand why she didn't have any with her but I was happy to help.

I also asked if she had any light sticks, which she didn't. Fortunately I had some left. Her sister said jokingly, 'You have given her all the presents and not given me anything!' I laughed and gave her a big bar of chocolate. The ladies were very funny and I was glad I could help out. I gave them both a hug and wished Yesenia all the best. I heard a couple of days later that unfortunately she didn't complete the swim due to the currents being very strong, but she put in a great effort.

John, Gemma and I had a long drive back towards John's house and our plan was to stop around halfway and stay at a hotel on route. We went to dinner that night at a traditional Japanese restaurant that served what the locals call *yakiniku*, which involved cooking your own raw meat and vegetables on hot plates. We had our own private booth and every time you required more food, you rang a buzzer and the waiter would come instantly. It was delicious and a real highlight.

The next day John drove all day and we finally arrived at his house around teatime. I Skyped my parents when we arrived to tell them about the swim. They were of course really excited for me that I had completed another one of the Ocean's Seven.

I asked how the dogs were. My two dogs, Booie, a Newfoundland, and Lady, a golden retriever, were staying at a friend of the family's. My mum said, 'Yeah, they are fine', but it was too sharp a response and she didn't seem comfortable with the question, struggling to look at me.

'What's happened?' I asked. 'Is everything OK?'

'Yeah,' she said, 'Nothing to worry about.'

I know my mum – she can't lie, I knew something was wrong.

'Is it Booie?' I asked. She was the oldest. I had always loved all my animals equally over the years and worried about them when I went away. One of my cats, Tinky, had died when I was in Hawaii, which upset me so much that I went from elation to devastation the day after the swim, when I found out. I had the strongest bond with Booie out of all of them, and my mum confirmed my worst fear that she had passed away the day I had arrived in Japan. It hurts me now to talk about her in the past tense.

Booie was a major part of my life; she loved the water even more than I did. Newfoundlands are an old breed from Canada. Previously known as Viking bear dogs, they were used in the 1800s to pull boats ashore. They have a natural affinity with swimming and water rescue. They have webbed feet and actually swim breaststroke. Ever since she had been a pup, if there was any sign of water Booie would charge for it. To her it was the best thing on earth and to see the joy on her face was truly heart-warming. Only two days after swimming the English Channel I took her for a walk at a park. We reached a lake and I knew she would make a dash for it. I had her on the lead and tried to hold her back – well, I didn't try that hard, to be honest, as I loved to see her paddle; it made her so happy. She dived straight in and I realised she couldn't get out unless she swam across the lake, which was at least 30 metres long. I didn't know whether she was capable of that; up until that point she had only done short swims. I started to panic a little so I jumped in with her and tried to lift her out of the water, but at sixty kilos this was easier said than done.

Booie was very happy being in the lake and made no attempt to get out. I seemed to be making things worse by holding her lead, and I soon realised that I'd do better to take her lead off and try swimming her across. I grabbed the lead with one arm and swam with the other, trying to help her in case she panicked or went under. After less than 5 metres of swimming with her, my feet sank into the mud. It felt like it was trying to suck me under; I only just had my head above water. I thought, 'I'm the one who's going under here!' I could just see the headlines: MAN SWIMS CHANNEL AND THEN DROWNS IN SMALL LAKE. I had no choice but to hold on to her and try to get my legs up before I was submerged. Booie gladly took on her role as lifesaver – what she was born to do. She pulled me in with the biggest smile on her face and when I climbed out, she turned back as if to say, 'Can we do it again, Dad?' I was so relieved she was OK, and she had really enjoyed herself.

A couple of years later, I joined a Newfoundland Club where they trained the dogs to do water rescue tests. I wasn't sure how Booie would react the first time. One of the members took her into the water and tested her retrieving skills. He first threw a ball and she brought it back, and he then tried a life ring – and again she retrieved it. I went out 25 metres and she swam out to me, and as she got closer she turned around as if expecting me to hold on to her, which I did around her rump and she pulled me back in. I then went out on a RIB with two other people and called her. It took another two people to hold her back – she was so desperate to come out to me. I dangled a piece of rope in the water at the front of the boat and to my amazement she swam out, grabbed the robe without any guidance and pulled us all in to shore. She was a natural and it was something quite remarkable to see. I hadn't taught her anything – her instincts led the way. There were a number of elements to each test, including retrieving a safety object like a life ring or rope, rescuing a person in the water from 25 metres away, swimming alongside someone for 25 metres without trying to jump on them, pulling a RIB back with people in it and dunking her head underwater to bring up a submerged rope.

We did six different tests together and she passed them all, but the most important thing is that she loved doing them and being in the water with me, as I did with her. At times, when I was out in a channel swim, thinking about Booie would help me focus and block out the negatives and I would visualise her swimming alongside me, smiling away, helping to distract my mind and drive me on. Even after she had gone, I believe I saw her face in the water a couple of times when I was training.

Booie was a remarkable dog. We formed a bond which cannot be replaced. I would give up every swim I've done in order to have her back. Swimming with her was the most enjoyment I've had in the water; I will forever miss my swimming soulmate and she will never be forgotten. I'm sure she was with me on my swims, willing me across.

The rest of the time in Japan was understandably sad. It is a beautiful place, but I just wanted to be home. Life is strange, sometimes, how you can go from such a high to an incredible low.

After ten days of tripping around, we arrived home and I went back to work a couple of days later. I was still very down about losing Booie and work was the last place I wanted to be.

21

TAKING
THE PLUNGE!

The swims were like escapism for me; they made me feel different and separated me from the crowd. The issue I had was that, without the swimming, I wasn't at peace with myself. I was now only two swims away from my ultimate goal and my priorities had changed. I knew I mustn't take my job for granted – without it I couldn't afford my swims – so it was crucial that I didn't allow my work to slip. I would have to carry on fitting my training in around the job, as I had done for the past few years, to ensure I was in good shape for the last two swims.

I'm sure to most people in the office the thought of swimming the Ocean's Seven didn't have any real purpose; that is the beauty of people – we are all different. I just knew I had to complete it in order to be happy. It is hard to put into words; I just felt that this was part of my life's script and there was some kind of unexplained force driving me on. I had to make it happen; I didn't have a choice.

I felt I needed to make a change in my working life; it was no good going back to work after a swim and feeling that I didn't belong. I had been talking to one of my friends, another Chris, who ran a local triathlon club, about the possibility of doing a swim camp at Colwick, Nottingham. This would be to teach swimmers my stroke technique as it was working really well for me despite the injuries. I knew I had something special, I had found a way to improve on my times and swim with more power and less effort, avoiding irritating the shoulder. I was confident others would take to it too so I set up two open-water swim training camps, which also covered psychology of open-water swimming.

Both camps had strong reviews and I loved it, starting to believe that this could be the job I was destined for. At university my friend Chris Rowley had told me I should become a teacher as I had a lot of patience and passion, and that had always stuck in my mind. I did some part-time swim teaching, which I loved to do, but I knew I couldn't live on the amount I was paid. People don't become swim coaches for the money, that's for sure, but the satisfaction you gain from teaching a life skill is a huge buzz and something I've always been very passionate about.

22

C-O-L-D WATER – NOT AS WARM AS WE WOULD LIKE!

My next swim, the Cook Strait in New Zealand, was due to take place sometime in 2015. I wanted to bring the date forward to early 2014 so that I could do the last one, from Ireland to Scotland, in August 2014. I contacted the organiser of the Cook Strait swims, a guy called Phil Rush, who was a very accomplished open-water swimmer himself. There was no way he was moving on the date. I tried bribing him with drinks as a joke, but I was stuck with 2015.

My only hope was to try to swap the date with Yesenia, whom I had met in Japan, as she too was aiming to swim the Ocean's Seven. As she didn't make the Japan swim, I politely asked if she didn't mind switching the dates with me and taking my slot in 2015 instead. She still had a number of swims left to complete the Ocean's Seven and I promised to help organise her Molokai Strait swim. She agreed and I was given the week commencing 21 April 2014. This was the latest possible date I'd be able to swim the Cook Strait as the temperatures drop to single figures in May. I knew no one had ever swum the Cook Strait as late as this, which gave me added pressure. I had hoped for an early date in January, when the temperature would be around 3 degrees warmer. I contacted Phil again to see if this was possible, and he replied, 'I would quit whilst I was ahead, if I were you.' Meaning I was lucky enough to have swapped and I shouldn't push my luck. I thought, 'Fair enough' – at least it would be a good test before the Ireland to Scotland swim, which was notoriously known to be the coldest of the seven.

I knew I had to train in colder water for the Cook Strait, as it could be as low as 14 degrees. As the temperature in the UK drops considerably once it gets to mid-October, my plan was to swim throughout the winter in water that would be cooler than the Cook Strait.

I swam each week in December, when the temperature had dropped to single figures. I remember arriving at my local lake in Lincoln after a few weeks of just swimming in the pool. There was a small group of ten to twelve people and when I turned up they said, 'It's Ocean's Seven swimmer Adam – he will swim all day in this!'

The temperature was 4.7 degrees centigrade – that's 25 degrees colder than a swimming pool! I had swum the year before in 5 degrees just once, and that was about all the single-figure swimming I had done. When it's this cold, under 5 degrees, it's called ice swimming. It is important at this temperature that the swim is well supervised, as you are at greater risk of hypothermia from the extreme cold.

I didn't know how my body would cope in the lake and I thought I had better fake this and not show weakness. There were some seasoned ice swimmers out there and as we were swimming around no one was talking, there was silence. Some were doing head-up breaststroke, not willing to put their faces in the water, and others head-up front crawl. My swim tactics were to convince myself I was enjoying it. As I swam past I chanted, 'Feeling hot, hot, hot!' After two or three times, the cold started to affect my speech and it sounded more like 'Fweeling huwott, ott, ott!'

There was method to my madness, though – I wasn't doing it to annoy the others. This method had worked when I was training for the English Channel; whilst I was saying positive words like 'hot' I couldn't be thinking I was cold. Everyone did one lap, which was around 250 metres, and I thought I would push myself for another. As I swam around the second time, I realised I was the only one left in the water. The problem now was that I had no one to sing and joke with and so my cold-water diversion tactics didn't feel as effective.

The others were changed and as I stepped out of the water I was helped by one of the guys I knew. I asked if he could help prop me up as I felt a little dizzy. The rest of the swimmers were dry and fully clothed and started chanting back, 'You're not singing any more, you're not singing any more!' It made me laugh. I hadn't faked it well enough and they were right: I wasn't singing any more! I looked like a bright pink lobster where the supply of blood to the skin had increased to try and keep the body temperature constant.

There are believed to be a number of health benefits from swimming in cold water. Scientists have found that it increases white blood cell counts and boosts the immune system, which can help prevent you from getting colds. It increases blood flow and can help with circulation and flushing out the system.

It also helps with weight loss, as you burn more calories in cold water than you do in warmer water, as the body is having to work harder. In addition it's good for stress and depression as it gives you a natural high. There are, though, obvious hypothermia risks associated with swimming in very cold water, which I know all too well. This is why only people with plenty of experience, who have built up to it through lots of small dips, can be confident and know their limits.

Every year there are Boxing Day swims up and down the country, which are designed to be fun, people often wearing Santa hats over their swim hats. Adults of all shapes and sizes challenge themselves to a small swim in icy temperatures in nothing but swimming trunks, hat and goggles. There is always a lot of safety on standby to ensure there are no problems. This same year I attended a Boxing Day swim at the Lincoln lake, with over a hundred people turning up for a dip. The choice was a 175-metre loop or, for the more experienced swimmer, 450 metres. There were a few frozen bodies when people got out but no major issues, thankfully.

The cold-water training seemed to really help: when it started to warm up in March it was 9 degrees (the temperature I had nearly died in when I first started) and I swam for around two hours without a wetsuit and was pretty comfortable. I thought how things had changed; I now saw the benefit of acclimatisation and all those dips I had had over the years, as well as the mental strength that comes with experience as it is no longer a shock to the system – the body and brain don't go into panic mode. I do believe weight also helps by providing an insulated layer to protect your major organs from the cold, which is why seals have blubber, but it isn't the major factor, as I have proved.

It was April before I knew it. This time I didn't have the issue of trying to raise the money as I had carried out a motivational talk to a company called TSYS (Total System Services) and the director, Kelley Knutson, very kindly agreed to sponsor me, which meant I could focus my full attention on training and it was one less thing to sort out. I tried everything to keep the costs down as I wanted to ensure something was left over for my final swim from Ireland to Scotland.

I was advised to fly out to New Zealand a week early in order to get over the jet lag. I knew I had to attempt the swim before the end of April to have any chance. I gave myself a few days before the start of the tide, having learned my lesson from Hawaii and Japan, where I had pretty much arrived and then done the swims after long flights.

23

SWIM #6 COOK STRAIT – A LITTLE HELP FROM MY FRIENDS

The flight to New Zealand was twenty-five hours long and though I considered breaking it up, I thought ultimately it would be best just to get there and settle into the time difference as New Zealand evening would be morning in the UK. We arrived in Wellington and my priority was to rest, which I'm not very good at doing. The prospect of a big swim like this never leaves your mind fully. I could park it at the back of my mind but it was important to stay focused and remember that, while I was over there, I had a job to do and success was the only option.

The hotel in Wellington was called At Home and I had found it on the internet. The hosts, Dwayne and Hayley, were two of the nicest people I could have wished to meet; nothing was too much trouble. Gemma was with me and we did feel at home being there – it was a great place to relax. We explored our surroundings and I was anxious to meet up with Phil to understand our chances of going. He had explained to me that there were very few swims possible each year due to the high winds and rough conditions you can encounter on the Cook Strait. I knew I may have to go on a fifty-fifty weather decision, but I was used to that from some of the other swims.

The first day, I did an easy thirty-five-minute training session and we found a nice swim spot. The sea was rough and windy, as predicted, and I was more conscious of the sea temperature than I had been since the English Channel. I gradually walked in and it didn't feel warm, but I told myself, 'This is manageable.' As I swam out, I started to think about sharks, for some reason. I didn't realise at the time that the Strait is known for having migrating great white sharks passing through. As I looked down into the murky water, I kept seeing the water cut up underneath me, but I put it down to my imagination and just swam on. The media was notified of my swim and they came to do an interview a couple of days after we arrived. They wanted to ask Phil about the potential challenge I would be facing.

It was 20 April and the best possible day to go would be the 22nd, four days after my arrival. There was no guarantee, though, as there had been a cyclone that had caused horrendous winds and stormy weather in recent weeks, so the ocean was still trying to recover. I hoped and prayed we could go. I didn't want to have to find the airfare to return and I would have to wait another year to complete the Ocean's Seven, which would be very disappointing.

Phil was planning to ring me on the afternoon of 21 April. It is so hard waiting to find out if you are going or not. The devil on my shoulder is always trying to say, 'If the weather is bad you have a way out', and the angel is saying, 'It's just another swim – let's go and get it done!' Phil rang as promised and confirmed that we would be going; there was a sense of excitement among the nerves that I had now experienced a number of times.

Phil had told me about there being three currents, and how it can be impossible to cross if the currents go against you. I chose to ignore this, playing it down in my mind and telling myself it would be a short, straightforward swim. Once again I felt I was due for a bit of good luck, especially after everything that had happened on the other swims up to this point – however, I had thought that in Japan too!

Gemma and I were due to meet Phil and the crew at the harbour for 6.30 a.m. It was around twenty-five minutes away and we left the hotel around 6. I decided to drive as I thought it would keep my mind occupied. We arrived at 6.20 a.m. in darkness and were ready to go. We packed everything we needed for the swim on board the boat and made our way out to the start point. Warm clothes, spare goggles, swim shorts, food and drink.

I was now becoming really sick of powdered carbohydrate drinks; I couldn't get used to them in training. My stomach wasn't coping with regularly consuming 350–400 millilitres every half hour or hour, and would reject it. On the channel swims themselves, it's hard to determine what caused me to be so sick; it could have been motion sickness, physical exertion, the drink or a combination of all three – I can't say for sure. During the Gibraltar Strait swim, I had taken regular carbohydrate powder drinks and been fine, with reasonable sea conditions. On the Catalina Island swim, however, I had experienced good sea conditions and yet been extremely sick. The sickness could have been triggered by being disorientated at swimming in darkness at the start, or by swallowing some water.

Gemma had made the suggestion of preparing a homemade soup of carrots, parsnips, tomatoes, onion and chickpeas, all blended up into a baby-food type of consistency. The benefit of making the soup yourself is that you can control what goes in, so it still has carbohydrates, albeit not as much as the powder. (I questioned whether I needed such a dosage of carbohydrates anyway, especially when my body would reject the powdered drinks so quickly.) Gemma didn't add any salt as this is the last thing you need when swimming in salt water – the sea is full of it and you take it on without even realising. I agreed that the soup was a good idea as there was nothing artificial in it, which gave me a positive association, unlike the powder. Phil also brought some non-flavoured carbohydrate gels with him as a backup. In addition I bought a few energy drinks I liked the taste of and which Dan Abel, an open-water swimming friend of mine, used on his swims. They had 30 grams of carbohydrate per 500 millilitres, which was similar to one scoop of the powder. I was concerned, though, as they were high in sugar and I hadn't used them before so I had no idea how my body would react to them. I also bought some simple quick-energy foods such as chocolate and sponge cakes, as well as flat Coke in case I was sick – it had worked so well in the past to settle my stomach.

I knew I still wasn't getting the nutrition right and there must be better, healthier, more effective alternatives for fuel. There is research to show the benefits of fat stores as a source of energy in a marathon swim. The argument being, you have thousands of calories stored in your body and would not run out, so the energy is consistent. Whereas you have to keep refuelling on carbohydrates to prevent depletion and energy lows. I do not yet understand enough to argue the point extensively, but I know there isn't one solution that works for everyone; I continue to keep an open mind.

On the boat ride out to the start of a swim, I always feel my mind is vulnerable to negatives and self-doubt, which I am aware of, and this is why I try to avoid complete silence, keeping my thoughts occupied with positivity, joking and motivation. The journey to the starting point was one and a half hours and I tried joking with Phil to keep myself relaxed and calm. I also listened to my motivational CDs, as I had done before previous swims. I feel these are my best weapons for combatting the devil on my shoulder.

Just before I slid into the water at Ohau Bay, the start point for the swim, I was sick over the side. It was probably due to motion sickness and a few nerves. Phil told me not to worry and just to get it out of my system. This was the first time I had been sick before the start of a swim. He also asked, 'What are you wearing around your ankle?'

I replied, 'It's a shark defence unit.'

'Why have you got one of those on?' he asked. 'There aren't any sharks out there!'

'Just in case.'

He said, 'I would rather you not wear it as it will be a distraction.'

I wasn't sure whether he meant to me or to him, but I did as I was told. In Hawaii I had felt happier mentally having it on in shark-infested waters – while the little green light was on I felt I had some sort of protection. I knew there were sharks in the Cook Strait despite what Phil said, but once again I hadn't read too much about this swim in order to keep my mind focused on the positives. I now know the Cook Strait's depth is on average 420 feet and that, due to its unpredictable waters, sailings and ferry crossing are occasionally cancelled as the Strait is too dangerous to cross. There have been a number of ferries that have capsized on it due to the conditions, resulting sadly in loss of life.

I entered the water at 8.10 a.m. As expected from testing the water temperature in a training session, it wasn't warm. It felt quite a lot colder than the English Channel. Phil said it was around 16 degrees centigrade, which must have referred only to the deceptive surface temperature; deeper down it can drop off significantly. I tried to put my face in and received a sharp pain across my forehead; it took me a few goes to keep it fully immersed. From experience, this normally occurs in 13–14 degrees with me. I switched off thoughts about how cold it was and started getting into my stroke.

As on my Gibraltar swim, my support crew, Phil and Gemma, were on a RIB next to me. The main boat with the GPS was leading out in front, which I much preferred; it meant that they could work out the currents and establish the best route for us to follow. This was the same as the Japan swim, where it had worked really well.

I was tense and once again I couldn't decide which side of the RIB to swim on. In the first thirty minutes I switched from breathing right into the RIB to left, then back again. I knew I was more comfortable breathing to the right and just needed to stick to it and stop messing around.

I noticed both Gemma and Phil had put jackets on; I kept thinking it must be cold outside. Gemma had her hood up and was wearing a number of layers of clothing. There was a strong wind and it started to rain. There was quite a swell but I kept thinking it wasn't as bad as Japan. A wave suddenly rolled over the top of me, breaking on the RIB and splashing them. I started smiling as I thought, 'Serves them right for looking so warm!' I was determined to try to enjoy the swim, and smiling even if you don't feel cheerful can really help deflect your worries. Phil gave me the middle finger and we both started laughing.

I had a fast pace for the first hour, covering 4.3 kilometres, but my mental state made me physically tense and my new stroke was all about relaxing and consuming as little energy as possible. Phil knew I wasn't at ease and he said, 'Now listen, you've covered four-point-three kilometres: you are doing really well, but just relax! If you don't relax I'll have to smack you over the head with my paddle!'

It was meant in a joking way but I wouldn't have put it past him. I have a lot of respect for Phil – he was a great swimmer in his day and has also coached to a very high level.

I had a small cup of the energy drink I had bought at the supermarket and carried on. I started to ease the pace down, like Phil said, relax my shoulders and get back to my normal swimming posture, with my head in a neutral position, looking downwards, and my eyes forward. By looking upwards, as I used to, I had quickly given myself a stiff neck and affected my body position, driving my legs downwards. This was how I used to swim and the reason I still have a nerve problem in my neck now. By looking downwards, the head is neutral and it takes pressure off the neck and spine. It also brings the hip and feet up, making the body more streamlined without the use of leg kicks, which saves a lot of energy.

I was annoyed at myself for the lapse in concentration and went back to swimming the most efficient way I knew how.

Instantly it took the pressure off, I felt more relaxed and it became easier again. A few minutes after my feed, Phil gave me the thumbs up as I was swimming much better. I felt a little tired and lethargic, though – I was swimming well enough but my legs felt like jelly. I thought it must be the jet lag and told myself it would pass. At one and a half hours I had some of Gemma's soup, which tasted amazing, and Phil said I was swimming much better.

It started to go wrong at the two-hour mark. I came in again and just after having some sports drink I turned my head into a wave and accidently swallowed a mouth full of seawater; within thirty seconds I started to be sick. As I've mentioned previously, I have been sick many times on these swims; it has unfortunately become common practice and as soon as I start it takes a good while for me to stop. I try not to get fazed or shocked by it any more as I know eventually it will pass. I try not to pre-empt it in my mind, but unfortunately it has simply become part of me doing a channel crossing.

For the next half an hour I felt I had even less energy; it didn't help having to slow down to be sick and then continue swimming. I couldn't allow the sickness to have power over me, so I tried to keep pushing through it and not stop for too long. I also didn't want to highlight any concern to the boat as I didn't want them to think I was in trouble and potentially ask me to exit the water out of fear for my health and safety. I was also anxious not to worry Gemma, though she was probably immune to worry after the last swim, when she had seen nature throw everything it had at me.

At the next feed stop, after two and a half hours, Phil seemed upbeat and happy. He said, 'You've covered ten kilometres –

I'm expecting in the next thirty minutes to be halfway.'

Even though he was upbeat, I still wasn't feeling great. I was given one of Phil's carbohydrate gels, which had been diluted with water. I saw him stirring the drink with his finger and thought, laughing to myself, 'I don't want to drink it now he's had his fingers in it!' He did this again another time and I told him to please stop putting his fingers in my drink; he responded by pretending to spit in it. You could have a joke with Phil, which really helped me to distract my mind from focusing on how bad I was feeling.

He does have his own ways of doing things, though, in order to get you across. For instance, if any coaches go with a swimmer to do the Cook Strait, they have to stay on the main boat and not on the RIB with Phil. The reason is that he wants to have full control of guiding and supporting the swimmer across as he believes it would be confusing to hear two voices and potentially mixed messages. On this occasion, Gemma was allowed on the RIB with him, but she could tell he didn't want her saying too much. If you want to book this swim, it has to be through Phil if it is to be official – there are no other organisations that are recognised for this crossing.

Phil passed the drink to me and unfortunately I vomited it up again. I knew it always took a while for the sickness to stop once it had started, so I had to be patient; I just felt so weak! For the next thirty minutes I slowed right down from lack of energy and I was just praying for it to pass. At hour three he tried some flat Coke, which had been my saviour in the past. When I came in I told him, 'I just had a rubbish thirty minutes!' I was starting to think I would have to swim the whole way feeling weak and sick. I swam off and was sick instantly from the Coke, which had never happened before. I was fed up with how I was feeling – I couldn't get any rhythm as I was being constantly interrupted.

I pleaded to the ocean gods in my mind, as I had done at my low point in Japan. I said, 'Please let me just finish without any problems – haven't I been through enough? Just give me something positive on these swims. Surely that's not too much to ask?' It had worked before and I felt comfortable talking to the ocean as if it were a person. I had developed a love/hate relationship with her throughout the swims – it could be my best friend and then at other times my worst enemy. The ocean gods would decide my fate on the day and all I could do was keep putting one arm in front of the other until I ran out of water.

Suddenly, as if my call were being answered, I saw a glimpse of a fin powering towards me, then out of sight. It was so quick that it was impossible to make out whether it was a dolphin or a shark. The only sign I had that it was a dolphin was the laughing and 'Woo!'s that came from Phil and Gemma on the RIB. I'm sure it would have been a different reaction if it had been a shark. Suddenly I was surrounded by dolphins – there were at least twelve of them. It was amazing, and beyond magical after all the challenges I had gone through; they were all worth it just for this moment. It was remarkable – they fell into a diamond formation with me. There were a couple directly in front, a few below and some on either side. At first I thought they must be curious to check out who or what I was. It was incredible how close they were to me: the ones in front were literally within touching distance, 2 or 3 inches away from my fingertips. I was anxious not to touch them and so I started swimming wider than normal to avoid them. I now had my very own unique training partners and the feeling was hard to put into words; it was extremely emotional. My heart was beating really fast with excitement. Sharing their world was such an honour. When I had wished for something positive to happen, I could not have imagined I would be given this unforgettable gift. I wondered whether this was some kind of reward from the ocean gods for having passed their tough tests up to now. For the previous five swims I had raised thousands of pounds for whale and dolphin conservation and had become passionate about the protection and wellbeing of these amazing mammals and now I was sharing the water with them.

I felt really mentally tuned in with the dolphins, as if we shared a mutual respect and common understanding through swimming together. We couldn't communicate vocally, but they were happy to be so close to me and I felt the same way. There was something very right about the situation I was in. I felt completely at ease and the tiredness suddenly seemed meaningless – even the swim didn't seem important at that moment. This was man and nature at its simplistic best, no small tank keeping them restricted, no overcrowding just me and them.

The pod drifted forward at my speed and one dolphin kept circling around me over and over, each time getting closer as if he or she wanted to make contact with my hand, but then wasn't sure. I felt a little dizzy as I swam mesmerised, looking in front of me and from side to side. I didn't want to miss one second of this interaction. It wasn't until I felt my neck getting sore after thirty minutes of doing this that I realised I had better start looking downwards again to take the pressure off it.

As I did this, I got a terrible shock. There was a shark

approximately 5 metres below me. It was moving slowly and gracefully, its tail and body swaying from side to side, drifting along. It was hard to tell the actual size of it as it was a few metres down and the depth can be deceptive, but I would say at least 6 feet long. I had a choice: I could focus on either the shark or the dolphins. I chose to focus on the dolphins and the magical experience I was having. I had worked hard in training and the swims themselves to find a way to channel discomfort and pain and to keep my mind positive, free of concerns. This was no different: I needed to focus on the positives. I diverted my eyes back to the dolphins and pretended I hadn't seen the shark. I tried not to think that it was a potentially dangerous situation, deciding not to inform the RIB either so that I did not raise any alarm. I didn't want them to pull me out when I felt so well shielded by the dolphins. I couldn't allow my mind to wander, as it served no benefit; I had experienced previous shark sightings in Japan and Hawaii, where I stayed calm, so I knew I must do the same here.

The reality is I swim in the ocean, where there are sharks – it is their home. I choose to be there. When you look at the actual facts, there are higher risks in my day-to-day life than being attacked by a shark. I think they are amazing creatures and quite misunderstood. I believe human beings have created this negative image of them through films, which have made us fear them. I don't believe a shark would actively hunt a human as we are not their normal food source; attacks may well happen from mistaken identity. I appreciate it is a very subjective view, but on the Cook Strait it helped me to keep a clear mind and to carry on with a swim that I had worked so hard for. Whatever the debate about sharks, I know the risks when I enter the water and I'd have no complaints if something did happen to me through a marine-life attack, intentional or otherwise. It is a risk I am willing to take to fulfil my dream and live the life I want to lead. There are risks every day that we choose not to concern ourselves about – we don't know what's around the corner and if we are afraid to do the things we love, we won't be happy. The important thing is how we deal with these fears in our minds, judging if they are a true threat or if we have convinced ourselves otherwise. When people cross the road, they don't pre-emptively worry, 'What if I get knocked over by a car?' They just cross it. Similarly, you cannot afford to overanalyse ocean-swimming. It's about keeping it simple, thinking positively, embracing your effort and making sure you do everything you can to keep each arm going over until you reach land and complete the swim.

I didn't look down much after that, and after a while I noticed at a glance that the shark wasn't there anymore.

I stopped for a drink on three and a half hours and I was convinced the dolphins would get bored and swim off. Amazingly, this wasn't the case: they stayed with me until I had finished my drink and then continued on. Phil joked that there would be an extra charge for this. He spoke back and forth to the main boat via radio about how incredible it was to have them there, and for so long. In all the Cook Strait crossings that he had been a part of (just over ninety at that time), he had never experienced anything like it. Gemma had never seen a dolphin at all and was absolutely blown away. She had taken three different cameras with her on the RIB and took a few photos on her mobile phone to post out to Facebook for those who were waiting for updates.

I still felt lethargic, but the dolphins had given me an amazing extra boost and kept my mind occupied. The next thirty minutes were again magical. The dolphins remained with me; some went to play with the main safety boat, which was behind me now, and they carried out a real show of flips and somersaults, which the crew thoroughly enjoyed. But there were always at least two or three with me the whole time; I was never left fully alone. I became more confident about positioning my arms and hands where they would normally be, realising the dolphins knew exactly where I was and that they would just pick up the speed to avoid me touching them if they had to. I treated them as training partners who I was trying to get to pick up the pace, and they reacted accordingly – still in front of me within inches, they would just do an extra flick of the tail to stay ahead.

Conditions were a little choppy, although I had been through much worse in Japan, so again it was about putting it into perspective and keeping a positive mindset. A wave came over the top of me at one stage and I tried to swim with it; I picked up speed and I was literally over the top of one of the dolphins, and as I came down again there was an effortless small flick of the tail to stay ahead. I felt very slow next to them. I was swimming alongside perfect swimming machines who can reach up to 30 miles per hour, five times faster than an Olympic sprinter in a calm pool. I still had fun trying to race them, although there was only going to be one winner. The dolphin that had been circling me from the start came so close that it touched my hand with its tail. I also had others come from different directions, determined to get as close as possible.

In addition to the dolphins, I also had a very large albatross floating near me, just far enough away for us both to feel comfortable that we wouldn't approach each other. I didn't fancy wrestling it in the middle of the channel – there was enough excitement with the dolphins. On the next feed another thirty minutes later, the dolphins again waited for me. It felt as if they sensed somehow that I needed the support. I wondered whether there was anything else going on below, like more sharks that I couldn't see and chose not to focus on. Although Phil had insisted at the start of the swim that there were no sharks in the Cook Strait, I found out later that he told tell Gemma about one occasion where a shark had eyeballed a swimmer who was attempting it and she had to climb out for safety reasons.

After another feed and an hour and a half of the dolphins swimming with me, Phil said, 'We've lost thirty minutes from you looking at them – ignore them. I know they are distracting.' It was said in good spirits and I know he was right, but it was just so difficult to not focus on them. This was one of the greatest moments of my life!

I started to think about my stroke technique and I said in my mind, 'Thanks, dolphins, for all your help, but I really need to focus.' I didn't want to think that and I regretted it instantly, as within a matter of seconds they disappeared and were gone. It was almost as if they had read my mind and knew their job was done. I selfishly wished for them back, but it was too late. I will never forget the time I shared with them – it will never leave me and will be imprinted in my mind for ever. It was a great privilege to share their water. I now felt I had more energy and the experience had given me a huge lift. Now more than ever I had to finish the swim after having the dolphins there to support me. I owed it to them as well as to myself.

I was now well over halfway and needed to get back into my swimming zone. There were smiles on the boat, though. I liked breathing towards the RIB and seeing Gemma smiling away; it reassured me that there were no immediate issues. I remember Phil telling me about the three separate currents to manoeuvre through and I was conscious of them throughout – apart from when the dolphins came, of course, which took all my focus.

I decided to feed on Gemma's homemade soup to settle my stomach; it was the only thing that I trusted not to make me sick. I still wasn't feeling like I was full of energy, but I was better than I had been a couple of hours earlier.

Shortly after the feed I shouted out, 'I've just seen a huge jellyfish!' The mood suddenly changed, and Phil shouted back in a concerned voice, 'Just, go, go, swim!'

I wondered what was wrong, but there was no time for explanation. I just instantly picked up the pace. I had been in this situation before and I was used to increasing the speed if necessary. I had no time to think about being tired now – it was a matter of head down and swim faster. When this had happened on the other channel swims I had kept a calm head; there was no panic and I had confidence in my stroke to pick up the pace. As I breathed into the RIB, Phil was waving his arm to push me on faster. He kept looking directly ahead as if there was some concern about where we were going. My thought was that the current was changing. The Cook Strait was going to stamp its authority to remind me why it had been chosen as one of the toughest seven swims in the world.

I started shouting to myself, 'Come on, Adam, come on!' I relished the challenge, I had discovered through these swims: I'm at my best when I'm up against it out there and have no choice but to push harder. Throughout the swims, I would tell myself, when this situation occurred, 'We will see how good you are now, and how much you want it!' I had a lot of confidence from the Tsugaru Strait and I thought, 'This is nothing in comparison to the last one – now don't think, Adam, and give it everything you have!' In one sense, not knowing how long and how far you have to sprint for is a good thing, as you can convince yourself it will be over soon and keep pushing through it.

It was very strange, but by sprinting I seemed to have more energy. After a while I felt like I had swum more than thirty minutes at this speed, but there was no sign of waving me in to the boat for a feed. I knew it must be important to carry on. I had a little glance up ahead and I could see slightly to the right of my eyeline some isolated rocky islands known as the Brothers, or to the native Maoris as Nga-whatu, which means 'the rocks'. There are actually two islands and a bunch of small rocks. They are now home to one of the world's rarest reptiles, the tuatara. Captain Cook's ship was nearly wrecked there in 1770 and a 41-foot lighthouse was erected in 1877.

The fear was that if the current took me to the west of these rocks, the swim would be over as I wouldn't be able to make it in to land. After a while I knew we must be making good progress as Phil was punching the air, looking a lot happier, and Gemma was smiling. It's funny out there in the ocean: as you are not communicating with the outside world for so long, you start studying body language and interpreting visual clues. That is why I would always advise anyone supporting someone on a swim that the best thing to do is look happy whatever happens, as the swimmer is analysing you closely, looking to work out the situation from your own reaction. If he or she feels that it's going badly they may give up, feeling it's a lost cause. On these swims you have to remain calm and positive and believe you are in control of your own destiny.

After an hour and a half of no feeds and constant sprinting, Phil gave me a hand gesture to say, 'Slow it down.' I realised then that we must be out of trouble. We came alongside the Brothers, and although we were right next to them, we were to the left-hand side and out of danger of being pushed out. Phil signalled to me again to come near the boat. He said, 'We have about three kilometres to go, and it's now straightforward to the end.'

It felt like the pressure was off, but I had been lured into a false sense of security so many times before, believing I was finished and then having to push hard again. When it comes to the ocean I have learned to not guarantee anything.

This time, however, there were no last-minute currents or alarm bells and at eight hours I had my final feed. Nothing could stop me now – it was the last stretch. 'Just one arm, then the other,' I would tell myself, as I had done so many times before.

The finish point for me was a sheer cliff face, a Jurassic-looking piece of rock on the South Island with no actual land to walk upon. As I approached the rocks I relived the same feeling that I had experienced on the previous five swims: it was one of relief and happiness that another one was ticked off the list. I tried to climb onto a sharp rock to get out. Gemma and Phil were shouting for me to come back, but I was determined to clear the water. I kept getting battered by the waves but I did clear it, grazing my leg in the process. It was acceptable according to the rules just to touch it, but I always want to make sure I clear the water if it's possible.

I swam back to the boat and climbed into the RIB. Phil took me back to the safety boat, my body was shaking due to the water temperature. I was mildly hypothermic. It had been a very overcast day and the air temperature didn't help.

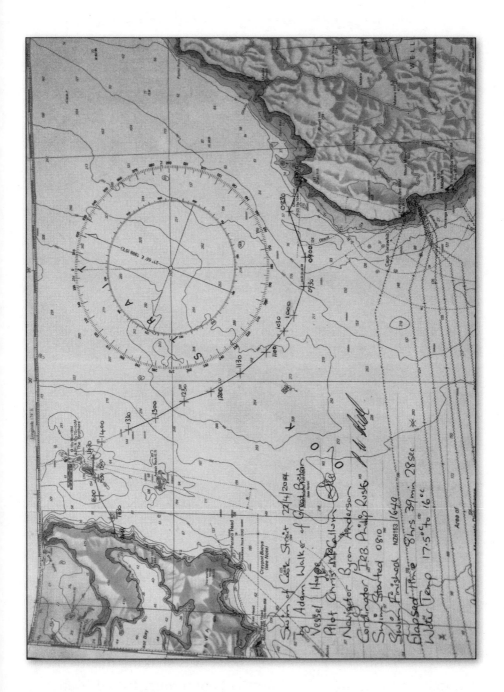

Crossing No: 92

**NEW ZEALAND
MARATHON
SWIMMING
FEDERATION**

Conquest of Cook Strait

This is to certify that

Adam Walker

*successfully completed the Cook Strait Crossing swim
consisting of 14 nautical miles*

from *North* *to* *South*

on the 22nd *day of* *April 2014*

In the time of 8 *hours* 39 *minutes* 28 *seconds*

*The swim has been duly entered in the
Record Book of the Federation*

_____ President

_____ Secretary

2nd May 2014 **Date of Certificate**

On the way back, Gemma showed me some of the pictures she had taken, including a dolphin in mid-air with me breathing to the side of the boat, which looked incredible. The whole day had been one I would never forget and I was truly blessed. I took a call from TV One, a New Zealand television channel, to explain the dolphin and shark encounter and that I had made the crossing.

It wasn't until we got back to the hotel that I told Gemma about the shark underneath me. She said, 'I'm glad I didn't know – I would have wanted you out!'

I told her I hadn't wanted to draw attention to the situation – there was nothing that could be done and I would have feared Phil taking me out of the water. We watched some of the videos of the dolphins swimming next to me that Gemma had taken, which were surreal!

The following day I rested and shared one of the videos with Danny Groves from the Whale and Dolphin Conservation charity, and I told him that it felt like the dolphins had protected me from a shark. (We will of course not know for sure as we don't speak the same language.) After sending the video, I didn't think anything else of it and went to bed.

At around 2 a.m. New Zealand time I received a call from a reporter at the *Daily Mail* back in the UK. He had also received a picture we had sent to the charity of the dolphin in mid-air as I was breathing to the side. The reporter asked me whether the photo was real as it looked too amazing. I joked and said, 'Unless my girlfriend left without me knowing in the middle of the swim and superimposed a dolphin into a shot, then its real.'

A few hours later I woke up again. Struggling to sleep, I thought I would check my emails. I was totally shocked when

I checked the video I had posted of the dolphins and saw that 25,000 people had watched it in two hours. I couldn't believe my eyes.

That same day we were planning to visit the South Island again – but to arrive by ferry this time! One perk of having swum the Cook Strait is that you receive a free ferry pass. That day, the video was watched by 1 million people across the world. I was so excited and pleased that all those people had seen how amazing the dolphins were to stay with me for such a long period of time. I hoped it would create some significant exposure for the Whale and Dolphin Conservation.

We stayed in the Marlborough wine area for a few days in a stunning hotel lodge owned by Heidi and Werner Pluss called 'The Peppertree'. We toured vineyards and a chocolate factory before travelling further south and exploring more beautiful places. These included Wanaka, an incredible town on the edge of a crystal-clear lake that is surrounded by snow-capped mountains. Gemma and I fell in love with the place.

The two weeks in New Zealand had been life-changing as a result of the dolphins. I don't believe it was just coincidence that they were there – it felt like they had assessed the situation and come to my aid. I also believe there is a deeper spiritual meaning to our encounter; it was more than just to protect me. I had to find out what that was. When I went back home to the UK, I couldn't stop thinking about what had happened and how fortunate I had been to experience them for so long. It had changed me in a big way and I knew I had to do more to help educate people about marine animals.

24

A BIG CHANGE FOR A BRIGHTER FUTURE

I went back to work with a new outlook on life and a strong sense of purpose. New Zealand had opened my eyes to what I was really passionate about and I knew I had to make some significant changes.

The first change was my job. I had been thinking about swim coaching full-time for a while and now was the perfect time. I had to follow my dream in my work life as well as in my personal one. Gemma had been made redundant by her company six months previously and we had been doing swim camps together for just over eight months. We called the business Ocean Walker – it was actually Gemma's dad who had come up with the name after joining us on a swim camp in Windermere. He noticed a book called *Fell Walker* in a hotel; he suggested the name in passing and, as obvious as it may seem, it just worked. I left Indesit with clarity and a real sense of excitement about what the future held.

I love swim coaching and I am very passionate about it. I knew from going on a swim camp myself six years earlier that it would be my dream job to run training camps, coaching and motivating people to achieve their dreams. I realised that I could do this in other ways as well as through swim coaching. I took part in a voluntary scheme called Skype in the Classroom and told my Ocean's Seven story to children in their classrooms and assemblies around the world. I began to receive enquiries for doing talks to schools and businesses, and it was an incredible feeling to know that what I had done so far could inspire people of different ages and different backgrounds to push for their own dreams and goals.

Leaving my job at this point seemed like good timing as I had just three months to go before my final Ocean's Seven swim, from Ireland to Scotland. It gave me the opportunity to train and put all my attention into getting across, which I had never had the luxury of before.

I needed to do an official six-hour swim in 13-degree water as part of the rules for the North Channel, the reason being that the swim itself would be in a similar temperature and I would potentially be doing twice the distance. It is important to assess people's capability for safety reasons and not to waste money and time.

I decided to travel to Scotland to do this as I knew I would get the colder water I needed in order to replicate the temperature of the North Channel; where I lived in Nottingham was 3 degrees warmer. Gemma, our two dogs and my friend James Wilson, who was also a swimmer, travelled to Loch Lomond. James and I planned to swim around Inchmurrin, the biggest island in Loch Lomond. I needed to do my six hours and he planned to do a couple of hours. The island is a kilometre-long circuit and would be a good test. We stayed in a lovely apartment on the island, which was only accessible by boat. The dogs were very excited to go on the boat and I had to hold Rosie back from jumping in. I knew if Booie, my Newfoundland, had been there I wouldn't have been able to stop her from throwing herself into the water and trying to swim across.

We arrived just before midnight due to a four-and-a-half-hour traffic jam. We did our first swim the next evening for one hour, which was so peaceful in the loch. I loved being in the quiet and able to just hear the water trickle as I swam; feeling isolated from the world. When I'm in the water it gives me so much pleasure and that never changes for me. I always have the same excitement getting in and feeling like I belong in there. It was stunning looking at the sky with the stars – at that moment there was no better place to be.

The following afternoon James and I did a two-hour swim together, which went according to plan. When I first started open-water swimming, two hours was a long time in my mind, but when you have done much bigger swims, such as ten hours plus, your brain tells you that it is nothing and you have no excuse to get out of the water until the time is up.

The third day was the planned six-hour swim, the main reason I had travelled all this way. I had a slow start to the morning. I can't say I have ever enjoyed a six-hour session, if I'm being totally honest, but I'm not sure there would be many people who genuinely enjoy being face down for most of the day in cold water. I had to tick this swim off, not only to qualify for the North Channel swim, but also because, mentally, it would give me an extra boost leading up to it.

Gemma came out in her kayak along with a bag full of goodies; she had made her vegetable soup and also brought some hot chocolate, water, sponge cakes and jelly sweets in preparation for our feeds. I did my normal talking to myself and joking with Gemma to deflect worried thoughts about the swim, and then I walked into the water. James decided to jump off the pontoon for a joke and came up gasping for air as the cold water took his breath away. I think he regretted it, by the look on his face.

I gradually waded in, trying not to think about the temperature and joking that it was warm and no problem at all. I had continued to use this tactic after Chris and I started doing it while training for the English Channel. Over the years I had told myself so many times that the water was warm, and although deep down I knew it wasn't I could trick my brain to thinking it was manageable. I joke that I have spent these last few years of training lying to myself and have created a false reality, albeit one that really does work.

The plan was to do kilometre-long circuits around the beautiful island. Everything was fine up until two and a half hours into the swim, when I had terrible stomach ache and desperately needed the toilet. I thought about swimming back to the cottage for a second, but I knew I wouldn't feel I had done a proper six-hour swim. I would have been disappointed and I needed to keep the positivity going leading up to my final Ocean's Seven swim. I had never given up on a training session before due to this issue, so I couldn't start now. After three hours, James got out of the water, which was the longest he had ever swum; a particularly great achievement in this temperature. He looked after the dogs and Gemma kayaked alongside me for safety. I completed the remaining three hours without too many issues and achieved my six-hour qualifier for the final swim.

For seven years I had heard from various experienced people in the open-water swimming community that the North Channel is the hardest swim of the seven, the main reasons being the extreme cold water and the lion's mane jellyfish. I did what I had done many times, which was to play it down in my mind and think back to the challenges I had survived in the previous swims. It couldn't be as bad as some of them. I decided that, whatever happened, I would make other swimmers aware that the North Channel is perfectly achievable, in order not to affect their confidence. It had always worked for me not to overthink the swims or put unnecessary pressure on myself. It was still the ocean and the same principles applied: one arm in front of the other and keeping a positive mindset. Again I told myself, 'If it's simple in my mind, it's simple in reality.' I really believe you get what you focus on. A big positive with the situations that I had to overcome on the previous six swims is that they had made me stronger mentally. Whenever anyone would say to me, 'Aren't you scared of being stung by lion's mane jellyfish?' I would respond with, 'It can't be as bad as a Portuguese man o' war!' This usually cut the conversation dead.

The Scottish trip was a short and productive one. I did what I had come to do, to get the qualifier done. Mental confidence is like a muscle: you have to work at it and the more you go through the stronger you become. What comes with experience is knowing your capabilities; if you have achieved your goals in training, there is less reason for your mind to create doubt about the real thing.

I returned home and balanced my training between swimming in the pool, the lake and the occasional ocean swim at Sutton-on-Sea in Lincolnshire, with my friend Anthony Plant, who was preparing for his first big swim, the English Channel. I did a few two- or three-hour swims in June and then went to Cork, Ireland, on a training camp. The camp is run by a very experienced swimmer, Ned Denison, and is designed to test swimmers to their limit, both physically and mentally. I went for the week and covered over 50 kilometres, including completing another three- and six-hour swim. I was purposely keeping the number of six-hour swims to a minimum after the Cook Strait, as even with the new stroke technique I was conscious not to overuse my bad shoulder since I now had one less biceps tendon fibre in my arm.

25

SWIM #7 NORTH CHANNEL – ONE MORE SWIM TO COMPLETE AN UNIMAGINABLE DREAM

My scheduled date for the North Channel swim was the week commencing 4 August. Gemma and I flew to Northern Ireland on the 1st. It was great to have a short flight of forty-five minutes and no time zone difference as I had with most of my other swims. We arrived and checked into a local bed and breakfast, which was just fifteen minutes' drive from Donaghadee, the start point for the swim.

We met up the next day with Quinton, my pilot for the crossing, so he could update us with all the details for the swim. I had a checklist of everything I could think of to ask about the swim; even though I had now completed six channels, there are always differences and each pilot has their own way of doing things. I immediately liked Quinton – he had a laid-back approach and made me feel instantly at ease. It is really important to me that I feel relaxed with the pilot and have 100 per cent trust in them, as I am in their hands for a number of potentially dangerous hours and they can make the difference between completing the swim or not. I had become a little more nervous after Hawaii – and, as it turned out, it was the best thing that happened to me, the reason being that I had to stretch myself and dig deep in order to finish the swim. I am grateful for how it turned out in the end.

Quinton came highly recommended as he had vast experience. He told me I should aim to finish within twelve hours, otherwise I was likely to be pushed back with the tide and would potentially have to wait another four hours for the tide to subside in order to reach land. I smiled; I had faced this issue many times on my swims and this was a normal obstacle in my mind. I had written down some questions which were comprehensively answered and I felt happy and relaxed.

I received the call on Sunday to say that there was no chance of swimming on Monday due to weather. Since we had arrived in Northern Ireland it had rained on and off every day, with thunderstorms and strong winds. Quinton phoned again on the Tuesday morning to say it was also looking doubtful for Wednesday, and if we didn't go before Thursday there was a good chance we wouldn't go at all. He agreed to phone again at 3 p.m. to confirm 100 per cent either way. When I received the call, he said the weather hadn't worsened and after checking again at 9 p.m. we agreed to meet at 6.30 a.m. on Wednesday, hopefully to swim.

I had originally planned for my brother Mark to come on the boat along with BBC television presenter Paul Bradshaw who was going to film the swim. I was concerned that, if the swim didn't go ahead, they would both make a wasted journey; it was a long distance for both of them to travel. I couldn't give either of them a definite response until the actual point of arriving that morning, after assessing the conditions and deciding whether to go for it or not. Mark said he would travel to Scotland the next day if I did end up doing the swim, and I had ultimately advised Paul not to come at all.

There was now a chance we would be going, so I had to focus my mind back onto the swim; nothing else mattered. The mental uncertainty that comes with ocean-swimming can be frustrating, I was now very experienced with this and I knew it was important to not waste any unnecessary energy. Although the swim never fully leaves you, a few days beforehand you have to focus your mind onto other things.

I decided, just one more time, to watch the movie that had triggered this journey for me and changed my life for ever. I had lost count of how many times I had watched *On a Clear Day*, but the movie always gave me such great motivation; I would watch over and over certain parts that inspired me to never give up. My favourite part is where Frank tells his friends in the middle of the English Channel that he wants to get out and give up. His friend then says to him, 'All my life I've looked up to you, Frank, all my life I never seen you back down from anything! You shut up about how much it hurts 'cos you don't have a choice – you never did!' I thought, 'I don't have a choice either – I never did! It is my destiny to complete this challenge, therefore I cannot give up.' I had repeated this line to myself many times in training and especially in Hawaii when I was in such agony during the Molokai swim, to keep pushing myself and to carry on no matter what.

I went to bed around 11 p.m. and listened to the same motivational CDs I had played over and over again during the last few years. They had served me so well in terms of keeping me focused and determined.

I didn't have a lot of sleep – maybe four hours or so. The alarm went off at 5 a.m. and I was full of anticipation that we would be able to attempt the swim.

We left at 5.40 a.m. and arrived at the boat in Donaghadee just before 6. Quinton's team were there waiting. He said, 'It looks OK at the moment – what do you want to do?'

I joked, saying, 'Another fifty-fifty chance of good or bad weather? Yeah, let's go for it!'

As in Japan, I went with my instincts. It really is hard to know what to do in situations like this; if I say no and wait for better conditions, I might not have another chance to swim for the rest of the year. Alternatively I say yes and the weather is too bad to complete the swim. The competitive side of me wants to say I'll take on a swim whatever the conditions, but the ocean is no place to be macho; if you are going to take it on you need a fighting chance, otherwise it will show its dominance and make you suffer. And the suffering is not always quick: it can be ongoing and energy-sapping, seemingly never-ending, and continue to punish you for hours.

We boarded the boat and set off. Mark was notified and I gave him the approximate time I would be arriving at the finish point in Scotland. It was all guesswork, of course; I didn't know whether the ocean gods would let me across, or what would happen along the way. I just had my faith and belief in my destiny to complete it.

It was only five minutes before we reached the start at Robbys Point. I got changed into my lucky shorts, which I had worn on other channel swims. I wouldn't call myself superstitious, but I guess there was some comfort in wearing the shorts that had got me across other big swims. Gemma once again donned a pair of rubber gloves and applied Vaseline to the back of my neck and my shoulders. I then said my thank-yous to the crew and in I went.

As I jumped into the water, the temperature took my breath away. I had been more conscious about the temperature of this swim than any other due to all the comments people had made to me over the years. I wanted to remove the thought from my mind, however, as I kept telling myself it was just another swim.

The North Channel rules were similar to those of the Tsugaru Strait: touch a rock to start the swim. Quinton kindly dropped me 10 metres away so I didn't have to swim far. I touched it and I was off. I thought, 'One more swim to go to complete the seven – let's get it done!'

A few minutes into the swim I saw the first of the lion's mane jellyfish and it was huge. The largest ever recorded was 7 feet 6 inches tall with tentacles 120 feet long. By comparison, the largest blue whale ever recorded was 108 feet long. I have seen plenty of jellyfish before, but the sheer size of them was something else. At least when I was stung by a Portuguese man o' war, I hadn't been able to see it in the dark. These jellyfish were not to be messed with; they looked like some kind of alien being.

I steered around the first few, gambling left then right, with the boat to my right-hand side. It was unnerving; I didn't want to have an encounter like I had experienced in Hawaii.

As I passed them, it was clear I wouldn't always have enough time to react and would most likely get stung. I decided to swim looking forward, which I didn't like doing as it hurt my neck and put pressure on my spine – the way I used to swim before changing it to the Ocean Walker technique.

After thirty minutes I swapped sides so that the boat was to my left, hoping there would be less of the jellyfish on that side. I had no idea, though – it was all luck and there was no way to tell where the best place to swim was in order to avoid them. Instead of Russian roulette it was jellyfish roulette, and losing would mean a very painful sting. The head of the jellyfish really does look like a lion's mane, but this part does not sting you; it is the tentacles that are loaded with stinging cells called nematocytes. The stings affects human beings in different ways, from painful rashes to blistering, muscle cramps, breathing problems and possibly even death.

Just before the first feed, I looked left and they appeared in my eyeline. I attempted to veer off to the right and then more appeared. I felt ambushed. I tried to think of a way out of there, but the only way out was to swim backwards, which wasn't ideal as I had not long started. I didn't want to spend most of the swim mentally blocking out jellyfish stings. I was more wary about them after the pain I had gone through in Hawaii, and although a lion's mane wouldn't hurt as much as a Portuguese man o' war, it would still be very painful. I didn't need any distractions so early into the swim.

I stopped swimming and turned around, lifting my legs as I did so and narrowly missing two behind me. The crew shouted out, 'What are you doing? Scotland is the other way!'

I said, 'Just getting away from the jellyfish!'

Another response back from Gary Knox, who was the observer: 'Just keep swimming – ignore them.'

Easy for him to say, I thought! I switched back to the left side, somehow narrowly avoiding getting stung once more.

I had my first feed on the hour, which was a new carbohydrate drink. We also had soup, but it was from the supermarket as our accommodation didn't have cooking facilities for Gemma to use. I wasn't sure how good it would be.

I was feeling the temperature more than ever before on a channel swim. I told myself I had swum in colder temperatures many times and I knew how to cope with it.

My concern was that, if I could feel it now, what was it going to be like in ten hours? I hadn't thought this way before and I'm sure it was ingrained in my subconscious from people being negative about this particular swim. I told myself, 'I am in control of the cold – it's all in my head.' I remember Quinton telling me it would get half a degree warmer after a couple of hours. I convinced myself that this would happen and so that was the first target to overcome.

I had a constant concern over the jellyfish stinging me, which I had never thought so much about before. I was finding it tough to relax, which I knew was burning unnecessary energy. There was much more eventful marine life underwater here than in the English Channel. At times I saw what appeared to be fishing line floating around and I was told afterwards that these were jellyfish tentacles. What I wasn't aware of at the time – probably for the best – was that when the lion's mane die they shed their tentacles and these can still sting you. I mean, how unfair is that?! I had been warned that, when they turn upside down, their tentacles float upwards towards the surface and it makes it even more difficult to avoid being stung. I was very anxious to keep my legs up as high as possible so that they didn't catch any floating tentacles.

The sea conditions were flat, and the water looked like

molten metal. The grey sky reflected onto the water and with no waves it was great – just what I had wanted on the other six swims. Although this was a positive, it could also become a negative as I knew that if conditions were flat, the jellyfish might come up to the surface; when it's rough they normally stay down, making it easier for swimmers to avoid them. At the start of the swim, I had actually hoped for rougher conditions.

After a couple of hours I did feel like I was warming up. I'm not sure whether that was because Quinton had previously mentioned it would happen and I was focusing on that, or because it actually was warmer. The sun was now on my back, which again made a big difference to how I felt. I started to relax a bit more, although I was still mindful of the jellyfish. I needed to capitalise on these calm conditions and push on, as I knew it could change at any time. As I reached the six-hour mark, I could see the Scottish cliffs at Portpatrick. They looked so close that I thought I could make them in a couple of hours.

Only a small number of people had ever made the crossing and the world record time was nine hours thirty-four minutes, which seemed achievable at my current speed. Temperature wasn't an issue any more and everything seemed to be going according to plan.

But as I swam on I was suddenly faced with what seemed like a lot of oversized half ping-pong balls in front of me. They were moon jellyfish, and as I found out afterwards not harmful to human beings as their toxins do not penetrate the skin; they only go after other small marine life. I was unaware of this at the time, though, having never seen them before and not being a specialist in jellyfish. I shouted to the boat, 'Do they sting?'

The response back from Gary: 'No!'

I thought, 'Well, he's going to tell me that anyway.'

They were quite stunning to look at, transparent on the outside but inside they varied in luminous colour from violet to red, pink, yellow and many others.

I managed to manoeuvre my way through them, slowly dodging left and right. It was impossible to avoid them all as there were too many. They were bouncing off the side of my face, arms and legs. On one of my strokes, I scooped one up in my hand on the pull, and immediately dropped it back in. It was like swimming in an extra-terrestrial world. I eventually made my way through them and the excitement was over. Every few minutes I would pass lion's mane jellyfish and I began to realise that they normally came in twos, so if I saw one I would keep a close eye out for the other.

I felt it was now only a matter of time before I finished. The sun was still out and conditions remained good, and as I reached the eight-hour mark we now seemed very close. Gemma put on my favourite motivational music over the boat tannoy and I could hear it when I went to breathe. This really lifted my spirits. At one point she drew a picture of a whale on the whiteboard we had on the boat. This made me smile as I thought she was saying, 'Do it for the whales, Adam!' What I didn't realise was that she was trying to let me know that there were actual whales not that far away! I never saw this until afterwards as she caught them on camera.

At eight hours thirty minutes, I was told I had 3 kilometres to go, and at this rate it was very achievable to beat the fastest-ever crossing. This would be the icing on the cake and finish my journey off in perfect fashion. I picked the pace up and pushed for the finish. At nine hours, we were so close to finishing and I could see the lighthouse. The problem was that I was being pushed sideways to the east and I couldn't get in!

At nine hours thirty minutes I still wasn't close enough and the record had gone. I had a little smile to myself – I felt it was the ocean demonstrating its final dominance and having the last say.

In some ways, it was quite apt that the swim wasn't entirely straightforward – none of them had been. This is why they were so notoriously tough.

I thought it was now only a matter of time before I hit land as I was so close. Then, without warning, Gemma and Gary starting shouting, 'You have to go faster!'

'Why?' I said. 'What's wrong?'

The tide was turning and suddenly there was a look of concern from the boat which hadn't been there before. I thought, 'Not again!' I had seen that look before. I started pleading with the ocean gods, 'Please let me finish – it is too important. I have to complete this swim!' I was less than half a mile from the finish but I remembered Quinton saying the last part was the toughest; he'd told me about a lady who attempted the crossing and who, having come within 150 yards from finishing, was pushed back out and didn't make it to shore. I tried to get that out of my mind and focus on staying calm and turning up the speed again. I continued talking to the ocean: 'Don't you dare ruin it for me now!'

I sprinted for forty minutes and started breathing very heavily, wondering how much longer I could keep it up. Then, suddenly and again without warning, as if nothing had ever happened, the body language on the boat seemed to change back to normal and the situation was calmer again.

I saw a boat full of people behind me; they were watching

me finish. I was excited and I thought Mark must be on it. He had travelled four hours to see me finish off the Ocean's Seven challenge. He had been there at the beginning when I swam the English Channel and it meant a lot to me if he was there at the end.

Gemma had been in communication with him throughout the swim. As I approached the final 100 metres, the boat came alongside me and I saw he wasn't on board. I wondered whether he knew where we were, as the plan had been to finish at the lighthouse, which of course we had now missed. It turned out that he was on the cliffs near the lighthouse, trying to get a view from the top. He was with a reporter from a Scottish newspaper, *The Sun*; they had apparently knocked on the door of a manor house to ask permission to look out from the bottom of their garden. The reporter explained they were trying to find a man swimming from Ireland to Scotland.

As I approached the last 50 metres, Quinton pointed out a rock for me to swim towards and touch to finish the swim. The people on the tourist boat next to me were cheering as I swam towards it. There was a shiver down my spine and I felt quite emotional. This was it: the completion of seven years of desire and hard work – a goal that would never have seemed possible in my wildest dreams. Somehow I was going to complete a challenge that involved pushing myself physically and mentally into the unknown, having never been 100 per cent fit.

I had prayed for this moment and it proved to me that everything really is possible if you don't believe there are any barriers to achieving whatever you set out to do.

I reached the rock and touched it, then turned around with a big smile and gave the thumbs up. The swim was over! The

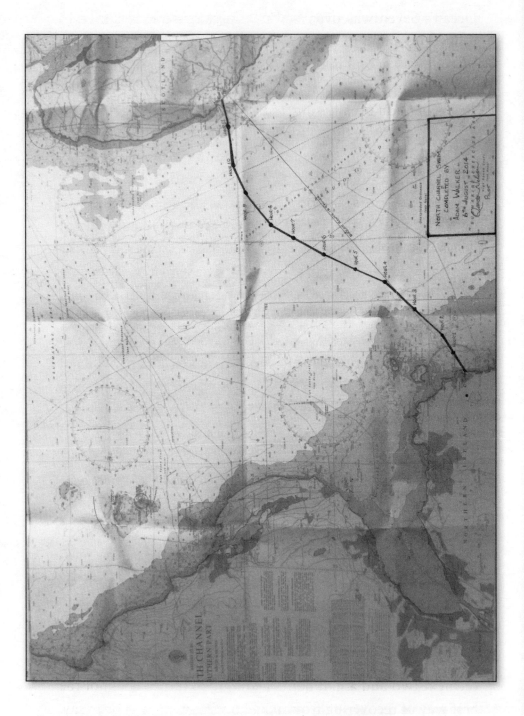

Ocean's Seven was over. It was a huge sense of relief. I had trained my mind to think I would achieve it and nothing but success was acceptable, but now it was done it was a little surreal. I had a calm celebration, as I had with the other swims; it hadn't really sunk in.

In fact, as I write this, it still hasn't really sunk in. I swam back to the boat and gave the crew and Gemma a big hug. I asked where Mark was as I wanted to celebrate with him. All my life he's been there and supported me, and it was fitting that he was with me at the finish. He had contacted Gemma and told her he was on land trying to get out to me with Chris Sweeney, the press guy. I asked one of the boat taxis if he minded picking them up and he said it would be his pleasure. Quinton agreed to wait until he came out, which was very good of him.

After forty minutes Mark arrived and it was a perfect end to my epic adventure. The heavens opened just before he got to me and it was raining very hard and chopping the water up. Maybe the ocean gods weren't so bad after all – they had waited for me to finish before becoming angry.

Before long we were all soaked. I hadn't realised that my clothes were on deck and were now saturated. I had just swum in freezing cold waters for ten hours forty-five minutes and now I had nothing to change into. I wrapped up in a robe and sat in my trunks inside the boat. I didn't really want to go inside as I would get seasick, but I needed to warm up. I had no choice. I sat inside holding onto the only other thing that was warm: a kettle. It seemed funny that I had left my job selling kettles because it wasn't my passion, and yet I needed a kettle more than ever now to keep me warm! I had to spend the next two and a half hours blanking out the cold – not the best way of recovering from a cold ocean swim, it's fair to say.

I arrived back in Ireland and thought, 'For the first time in seven years I have no Ocean's Seven swims left to think about . . .' Clem had told me to not think of each swim as the main objective in itself, but instead part of a process that would result in me achieving my overall goal. Each swim was not the be-all and end-all in my mind – it was just a small part of a longer-term plan – so I had never over-celebrated, always focusing on the next one.

I had expected to complete all seven swims and I am a firm believer that you get what you focus on. They say those who believe they can do something and those who believe they can't are normally both right!

26

CREATING YOUR OWN DESTINY

I had run out of swims and for the first time in years I could relax and enjoy my achievements. It felt strange as the pressure was now off. When I arrived home, it was a great feeling knowing I had achieved my dream. These seven channels were far more than just swims – they taught me so many lessons that I was able to put to practical use in my life. Each one presented its own challenge, which, like problems in everyday life, seemed at times impossible to overcome. I realised if I just stuck with whatever obstacle I was faced with, such as big waves and strong currents, at some point they would cease and I could then keep moving forwards. The answer was not to give up or accept that the barriers were more powerful than my desire to get through them.

I realised that the power of the mind is far stronger than a person's physical capabilities. You can do anything you truly want to if you don't allow self-doubt and fear of failing cripple you into making a bad decision or commitment. Nothing is beyond you and the world is full of incredible things that you can achieve. I urge you, if you have a burning desire to step out into the unknown and challenge yourself to find out what you are capable of, then listen to your thoughts and desires and do it. I believe there are often signs pushing you in a certain direction; for me and swimming, it was watching a movie on an aeroplane that changed everything, but it could have been any number of other prompts. I chose to take heed of that sign, but I could have ignored it and carried on being unhappy. Don't accept unhappiness – there are always options to change your circumstances and situation, but you have to create a different path by making a change and only you can make it happen.

When I took the hint and really looked at my life, I saw an unhappy future continuing on paths that could only get worse. I was looking for inspiration. On that day when I boarded the plane, I was without knowing it at my most open-minded, my most ready for change, and the movie made a connection with me. It offered a physical and mental challenge that would take me beyond my perceived limits. Swimming was a sport I was familiar with and one that represented a consistency that I hadn't had with other sports due to my injuries, but I was inspired to take it to an exciting new level and change my life for the better.

I don't believe I was born an open-water swimmer or that it is what I was put on the earth to do. At that time in my life, it was something I had to do in order to give me the happiness I craved so much. My relationship with sport had always been a strong one and I was always at my happiest doing some kind of physical activity, whether it was on the field playing rugby or cricket, on the tennis court with my brother, or in the pool swimming. This never left me as I moved into adult life, and so when I chose to go into a career in which a lot of my time was spent in an office or in front of a computer, it just wasn't the right fit for me.

I now look at the world differently and keep my eyes and ears open for opportunity. I believe the Ocean's Seven has given me much more than seven tough swims and an individual achievement. I now know the swims had to be completed in order to give me an opportunity to move on into new passions and meaningful causes, ones in which I could make a real difference. These will continue to give me the fulfilment I was missing for so many years. The swims are not the important part – what is important is what it all means.

For me, the swims are a metaphor for life: the struggles encountered, the sacrifice necessary in order to succeed, and the continued belief that you can pursue your dreams right to the end – no matter what barriers and pain you face.

27

FOLLOW
YOUR BELIEFS

In the short time following the swims the next phase in my
life had already begun. I finished the last swim in
Scotland on 6 August 2014. In March 2015, I travelled back
to New Zealand to be filmed for a documentary on dolphin
intelligence. I was so excited. Initially I was due to be filmed
for three days in Kaikoura on the South Island, and to do a
reconstruction of the swim in which the dolphins had come to
support me in the Cook Strait.

On the first day we arrived early in the morning at the
boat we had chartered for the day. I was bursting with
excitement to get back out with the dolphins and relive
those memories. We chose Kaikoura as they have the same
type of dolphin species – dusky – as those I had encountered
on my channel swim. They are very distinctive, with an
evenly sloped head, white belly, grey from their eye to
the flipper, and black on the tail and along the back. In
addition they have two white stripes that run from the

dorsal fin to the tail. They average 6 feet to 6 feet 5 inches in length.

It was a short boat ride out and they just appeared. It was like seeing old friends. I was ready to throw myself into the water, but the cameramen weren't ready. John Jackson, one of the directors, said, 'Adam, we are going to be swimming a lot today – don't worry, you will be doing lots of swimming.'

I laughed and in my mind thought, 'What does he class as lots of swimming?'

There was a short wait while the cameraman put on his dry suit and flippers. Getting ready for me consisted of swim trunks, hat and goggles – that's it. I had to be wearing the same as I had been on the actual Cook Strait swim. I hadn't owned a wetsuit – or worn one, anyway – since getting hypothermia on my first ever open-water swim in 2008.

We dived in with a small pod of around ten or twelve dolphins, which was very similar in number to the pod that had swum with me the previous year. As I jumped in, immediately I felt calm and at peace. For me, the ocean is such a relaxing place – I'm happiest out there where nothing else matters. Everyday life just doesn't seem important and if you then add dolphins into the mix, there is nothing on land to rival such an experience. There is something very right and pure about the ocean world and a dolphin pod that stick together no matter what they face. They approach life together and they are unconditionally loyal to the end. It is a world we continue to try to understand through science, so that we can learn from them. We must do this in the right way, observing them in their own natural habitats rather than putting them in marine parks or science centres where they swim around in small tanks living a miserable life just for our enjoyment. This is why the Cook Strait experience was so magical: they chose to be with me in their natural environment.

As I swam with them again, the memories came flooding back. We stayed in and filmed for just over an hour the first time, and then went back in another couple of times to get more shots. For three days, each pod would stay with me for only a short period of time and then move on. This demonstrated further how special and unique my experience in the Cook Strait had been, when they spent an hour and a half with me and even stopped when I did.

After the three days we travelled to Auckland on the North Island, and I interviewed a man who had had a similar experience to mine. He had been swimming in the ocean with his family when a pod of dolphins appeared and surrounded them. They were banging their tails on the water, which is one way they communicate to each other. His daughter and family were stressed as they didn't know what was going on, so he swam away from the pod to assess what the issue was. As he did this, a dolphin followed him and he looked down and saw a great white shark underneath him, which was swimming for his family. A few seconds later the whole experience was over. He said to me that he was very pleased the dolphins had been there and felt they had sensed the danger and treated him and his family as part of their pod, surrounding them in order to protect them. It was another example of dolphins potentially coming to the aid of a human being in the water.

After the New Zealand trip we travelled to Kona, Hawaii, to gain more footage of a different type of dolphin species called spinner. There are actually thirty types of dolphin, which vary not only in how they look but also in how they communicate; each pod has a different signature whistle.

This means that dolphins from different pods are not able to communicate with each other – it's rather like us humans speaking in different languages.

Dolphins also vary in intelligence, rather like people. The spinner is famous for its acrobatic displays. Its dorsal area is dark grey, its sides light grey and the belly pale grey or white. A dark band runs from eye to eye and to the flipper, bordered above by a thin line. The spinner can vary in form and colour, depending on where it is located. They are more difficult to find and are at this time considered to be an endangered species due to fishing – they get tangled in nets – plus pollution from chemicals and plastics.

As well as filming me swimming with them, my job was to interview two people who had swum with dolphins as part of a therapy programme. It was very interesting to get their perspectives on what it was about dolphins that had helped them. Both had answers that were very similar to mine: the feeling of being at one with nature and a sense of something honest and pure taking away stresses and strains from everyday life. Life's issues seem irrelevant when you're out there with them.

What happened to me in New Zealand had such a profound effect on me that it is hard to put into words. It was human and dolphin interaction, I believe as nature intended. I had a definite connection with them. We do know through science data that they possess a high level of intelligence. The documentary sets out to demonstrate all aspects of this intelligence, showing examples that will help the viewer gain a better understanding of the dolphin species.

If we look at scientific findings, a dolphin has an absolute brain mass of 1,500–1,700 grams, which is greater than human beings, who have a brain mass of 1,300–1,400 grams. This doesn't mean dolphins are necessarily more intelligent than humans, but it does mean there is more mass available for cognitive functions.

Here are just some examples of dolphin intelligence:

They demonstrate complex play by bow riding on waves.

They create bubble or vortex rings, often biting them to create lots of smaller bubbles that rise to the surface and form bubble nets for the purpose of foraging.

Their creative ability – from performing tricks to mimicking and copying each other.

Their self-awareness, from recognising themselves in a mirror to doing somersaults and playing.

Their innovative ways of catching food; they even create sponges that they wrap around their rostra (their 'noses') to use as a tool to help forage for food without damaging themselves, we assume.

They are known to help other species such as orca and other human beings – myself included. In Laguna, Brazil, for instance, a pod of bottlenose dolphins has for the past twenty years herded schools of mullet towards the fishermen near the shore; they then signal for the fishermen to cast their nets by slapping their tails. In return, the dolphins get whatever the fishermen discard.

As well as dolphins supporting humans, there are also examples of this relationship being reciprocated. During my trip I interviewed a lady called Martina Wing, who in 2013 had taken a video in Kona of a dolphin appearing to ask a human being for help. The dolphin had had its left pectoral fin snagged by a fishing hook and the line was coming across its mouth. Martina reported that the lone dolphin had swum in front of one of the scuba divers on the manta dive she was on, floating in front of him on its side to show the hook. The diver realised the problem and began cutting away at the fishing line to remove the hook. In between the dolphin would go up for air and come back to the scuba diver, appearing to sense that he was helping. The diver removed the hook and cut the line and the dolphin swam off.

We are halfway through filming now and already we are showing some great examples of the characteristics dolphins possess. My hope is that sharing our findings with the public will help us become more aware that marine parks and captivity are wrong. The film, *Conversations With Dolphins*, will be out in 2016.

Some countries are already making steps to forbid captivity. India's Ministry of Environments and Forests, for instance, has, on the basis of dolphin intelligence, forbidden the keeping of captive dolphins for entertainment anywhere in the country. The ministry has also made the bold statement that 'cetaceans in general are highly intelligent and sensitive and various scientists who have researched dolphin behaviour have suggested that the unusual high intelligence, as compared to other animals, means that dolphins should be seen as non-human persons and as such should have their own specific rights, and it is morally unacceptable to keep them captive for entertainment.' A paper proposing that dolphin rights be enshrined in law has not yet been approved, but the ministry have recommended the following:

1. *Every individual cetacean has the right to life.*
2. *No cetacean should be held in captivity or servitude; be subject to cruel treatment; or be removed from their natural environment.*

3. *All cetaceans have the right to freedom of movement and residence within their natural environment.*
4. *No cetacean is the property of any State, corporation, human group or individual.*
5. *Cetaceans have the right to the protection of their natural environment.*
6. *Cetaceans have the right not to be subject to the disruption of their cultures.*
7. *The rights, freedoms and norms set forth in this Declaration should be protected under international and domestic law.*

It would be a huge step in the right direction if the paper went through and it would hopefully set a trend for other countries to give dolphins rights and ban barbaric hunts.

Being involved in the film has opened my eyes further and made me more determined than ever to campaign for and support the freedom of whales and dolphins across the globe.

28

HERE'S TO THE FUTURE!

Open-water swimming has opened up a new world and so many possibilities for me. I have a lot to be grateful for. Although I really believe the movie *On a Clear Day* was the trigger that set off an idea, it inspired me enough to push towards a goal and not let anything get in the way of achieving it.

I learned more about myself in those seven years than I had in the twenty-eight years leading up to them. I discovered how important it is to find mental strength no matter what you are faced with, to decide your own destiny, and to fully understand that the only barriers to your success are the ones you create in your own mind. All you have to do is commit to something and do everything in your power to make it happen, and you can change your life for ever. I am a testament to that.

I am now doing the things I love to do. I continue to support the Whale and Dolphin Conservation (WDC) charity as a patron. I became the open-water swimming ambassador for the Royal Life Saving Society UK, the anti-drowning charity, helping to raise awareness of open water and how to enjoy it safely. Swimming is a life skill and it is essential we do not lose sight of how important it is. Through swim coaching I am teaching all abilities of swimmers the Ocean Walker technique across the world, as well as motivating others through talks to chase and fulfil their dreams. Working on the documentary has been a pleasure, something that I am proud to be involved with. It's not easy as you are not just handed amazing opportunities on a plate and have to work at them, as I had to with my swims, but the rewards are worth it, bringing happiness and fulfilment into your life.

I would have never dreamt that the seven swims would create this platform from which I am able to make a real difference. All I knew is that something was driving me on inside to complete them, and I had to make it happen!

I feel like I have been reborn and had a second chance at doing something I truly believe in. Dreams can come true; you have to just find out what you want to do, step over that line and 'Do it!'

So what's next? Good question.

I feel my purpose is to continue to support worthwhile causes and inspire others to achieve their dreams. I will continue to coach people my Ocean Walker technique, as I passionately believe this stroke will help redefine distance swimming. The improvements experienced by people from all around the world have been significant and I feel really excited for the future.

I will continue to challenge myself in various ways, which will include swimming. I will look forward to giving more motivational talks telling my story and hopefully inspiring others to step out of their comfort zone. I feel that life has endless possibility now and that really excites me.

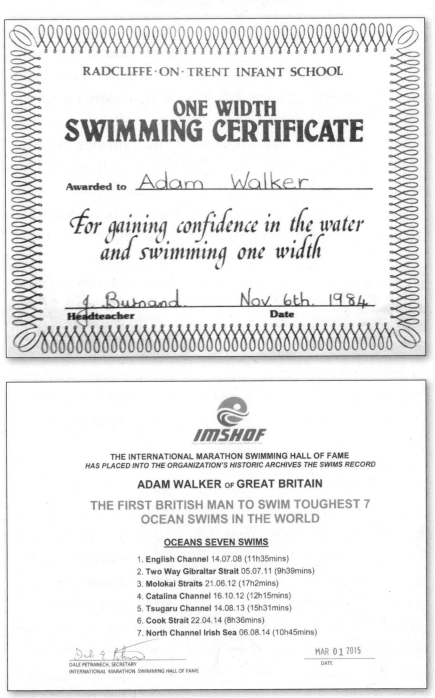

RADCLIFFE·ON·TRENT INFANT SCHOOL

ONE WIDTH
SWIMMING CERTIFICATE

Awarded to *Adam Walker*

For gaining confidence in the water and swimming one width

J. Bunand.   Nov. 6th. 1984

Headteacher   Date

IMSHOF

THE INTERNATIONAL MARATHON SWIMMING HALL OF FAME
HAS PLACED INTO THE ORGANIZATION'S HISTORIC ARCHIVES THE SWIMS RECORD

ADAM WALKER of **GREAT BRITAIN**

THE FIRST BRITISH MAN TO SWIM TOUGHEST 7 OCEAN SWIMS IN THE WORLD

OCEANS SEVEN SWIMS

1. **English Channel** 14.07.08 (11h35mins)
2. **Two Way Gibraltar Strait** 05.07.11 (9h39mins)
3. **Molokai Straits** 21.06.12 (17h2mins)
4. **Catalina Channel** 16.10.12 (12h15mins)
5. **Tsugaru Channel** 14.08.13 (15h31mins)
6. **Cook Strait** 22.04.14 (8h36mins)
7. **North Channel Irish Sea** 06.08.14 (10h45mins)

MAR 01 2015

DALE PETRANECH, SECRETARY   DATE
INTERNATIONAL MARATHON SWIMMING HALL OF FAME

I want the person who reads this book to know, whatever you choose in life, that it is possible. It doesn't have to be swimming or even a sport. There are no barriers except the ones in your mind. Dream big and know you will make it!

Never give up on your dreams!

ACKNOWLEDGEMENTS

A challenge like this cannot be undertaken without support from friends and loved ones. I have been blessed with many people who have helped me on my journey which I am truly grateful for and I owe so much to.

I would like to first give a very special mention to my girlfriend and best friend Gemma for not only helping me with the editing of the book but creating the front cover and supporting me throughout any challenges I came up against while writing it. In addition, I would also like to thank you for your support throughout my swims on and off the boat, which made it truly possible to achieve the Oceans Seven and my dream. I look forward to facing new challenges and fulfilling more dreams together. I love you so much and thank you for everything.

Also to my Mum and Dad for their ongoing support and guidance throughout my life, giving me every opportunity to follow my dreams and passions in order to shape the person I want to be. Also thank you to my Dad for instilling in me from an early age the need to push myself and give it my all in everything I do, it is now the principle I live my life by. I am very lucky to have such thoughtful, caring parents. Thanks, Mum and Dad.

Other big thank-yous:

To my brother Mark for all the help and advice you've given me over the years. For being someone I could look up to, providing inspiration and guidance along the way.

To my remaining family who have been there for me throughout.

Clem and Margaret Turner for not only supporting with hypnotherapy in all my swims, but in other areas of my life, lending your support unconditionally. You are two very kind, generous people with great hearts, always thinking of others.

Tracy Gjertsen at Physio Fit Lincs, Teresa Dixon and Colin Slaven. You certainly had your work cut out and I can't thank you enough for your treatment over the years, getting me in the best possible shape for training and the channel swims.

Dean Haspey at Sports Clinical, whose treatment has helped me across the last three channel swims and ongoing, for which I am truly grateful. Thank you for keeping me in one piece and being such a good friend.

Steve Munatones for creating the Oceans Seven.

Adrian Sington and all at Kruger Cowne; Lex Sheppard; Ann Nelson at Wanaka Heights Motel; Anthony Plant; Chris Sheppard; David Annand and Zoggs; Daron Vaughan; Dwayne and Hayley Watkinson at Home Hotel; Freda Streeter; Glenn Matsumoto; Heidi and Werner Pluss at The Peppertree; Hugh Hunter; Ian Johnson; James Wilson; Jim Boucher; John Raynor; Junior Vinano; Kelley Knutson and Grant Williams at TSYS; Libby Morley and Indesit; Linda Kaiser; Mike Dailey

ACKNOWLEDGEMENTS

and the Equus Hotel; Penny and Wilson Hogg; Pauline and John at Lime Tree Lodge; Richard Seals and Southwell Water Polo team; Rob Fergusson at David Lloyd; Roger North; Roger Soulsby; Simon, Neil and Will from Reckless; Stuart Parker and Jake Helm at Chelsea Health Club and Spa; Sue Murray; Terry Ellward; Tim Wright at Russell Hobbs; Toby Buchan at John Blake Publishing. Finally, Wayne Annan, Pauline Mills and everyone who has helped me over the years: thank you from the bottom of my heart.